Palestinians, Refugees,
and the Middle East Peace Process

PALESTINIANS, REFUGEES, and the MIDDLE EAST PEACE PROCESS

DON PERETZ

UNITED STATES INSTITUTE OF PEACE PRESS
Washington, D.C.

United States Institute of Peace
1550 M Street, N.W.
Washington, D.C. 20005-1708

First published 1993
Second printing 1996
Printed in the United States of America

The paper used in this publication meets the minimum requirements of American National Standard for Information Sciences—Permanence of Paper for Printed Library Materials, ANSI Z39.48-1984.

Library of Congress Cataloging-in-Publication Data
Peretz, Don, 1922–
    Palestinians, refugees, and the Middle East peace process / Don Peretz.
        p. cm.
    Includes bibliographical references and index.
    ISBN 1-878379-32-1 (alk. paper)
    1. Jewish-Arab relations—1973– 2. Palestinian Arabs. 3. Refugees, Arab.
  I. Title. II. Title: Middle East peace process.
DS119.7.P4523 1993
325'.21'095694—dc20
                                                                    93-37820
                                                                         CIP

Contents

Foreword

Of all the problems in the Middle East, the issue of the Palestine refugees continues to be one of the most intractable. And despite the dramatic events of September and October 1993 (Israeli recognition of the PLO, signing of the Israeli-PLO accords, discussions of limited self-governance for Palestinians), the refugee issue remains unresolved. Indeed, the increasing number of refugees has led to ever larger allocations of funds from the international community to UNRWA, the UN agency charged with refugee care.

Although some observers believe that resolution of the political issues will also lead to resolution of the refugee dilemma, others believe that the refugee problem will continue to be a source of regional tensions and instability regardless of the political outcome. What, then, are the practical issues that need to be considered now in order to deal with this dilemma? Among the issues that Don Peretz analyzes in this balanced overview are the current status of the refugees; the capacities of the West Bank, Gaza, and the host countries (Jordan, Lebanon, and Syria) to absorb the refugee population already within their borders as well as those refugees likely to immigrate from the surrounding areas; and the need for educational, health, and social welfare facilities.

In Peretz's view, the Palestine refugee problem cannot be resolved except as part of an overall settlement of the Arab-Israeli conflict. Issues such as the political identity of the Palestinians, the control of Jerusalem, and evaluation of and compensation for property taken or left behind will only be determined within the context of a peace settlement, as is also true of larger regional issues such as economic development, water resources, and the environment.

At the same time, Peretz also argues that it will be impossible to resolve the Arab-Israeli conflict without confronting the Palestine refugee question and the many related issues presented in this volume. His well-informed and informative analysis gives us a solid foundation for exploring ways to come to grips with these complex issues.

Don Peretz completed this book while a visiting fellow at the Institute as part of a much larger USIP effort to contribute to peacemaking and conflict management in the Middle East through research and education. In early 1991, the Institute established its Special Middle East Program in Peacemaking and Conflict Resolution as a vehicle for its own projects as well as to facilitate coordination with other Institute activities. These have included numerous grants, fellowships, study groups, and a diplomatic simulation, as well as publications such as *Making Peace Among Arabs and Israelis: Lessons from Fifty Years of Negotiating Experience* by Kenneth W. Stein and Samuel W. Lewis; *Arms Control and Confidence Building in the Middle East*, edited by Alan Platt; and *The Arab World after Desert Storm* by Muhammad Faour. All these programs contribute to the Institute objectives of providing information and supporting activities related to peacemaking and conflict management, and analyzing ways in which more stable local and international frameworks can contribute to the peaceful resolution of conflict.

Richard H. Solomon, President
United States Institute of Peace

Preface

This study of Palestine refugees and Middle East stability was undertaken in 1992 when I was a visiting fellow in the Jennings Randolph Program for International Peace at the United States Institute of Peace in Washington, D.C. My interest and involvement in the subject began in 1947–48, when I observed the beginning of the problem firsthand as a stringer for NBC; in 1949, I worked with Palestine refugees in northern Israel as a representative of the American Friends Service Committee (Quakers) with the United Nations Relief for Palestine Refugees.

Early on it became evident to me and to other observers of the Middle East that the Palestine refugee problem was one of the most critical issues in the area and that peaceful settlement of the Arab-Israeli conflict could not be attained without confronting the refugee problem. In 1952 I received a fellowship from the Ford Foundation to continue my study of the refugee problem. The results of this study were published by the Middle East Institute in 1955 as a book, *Israel and the Palestine Refugees*, and formed the basis of my Ph.D. thesis at Columbia University. In 1962 I extended this study under a grant from the Rockefeller Foundation; my observations were published in several articles in *Foreign Affairs, Middle East Journal, Jewish Social Studies, Orbis, Christian Century, Christianity and Crisis, Current History*, and other publications.

In my research for this and previous studies I made use of UN documentation; the Israeli, Middle East, and Western press; and extended discussions with Israeli, U.S., and UN officials; representatives of Palestinian organizations; and refugees themselves. None of the individuals or organizations consulted is responsible for the content or conclusions of this study; these are based primarily on my own observations and discussions with those involved.

The purpose of this study is not to engage in a discussion of responsibility for the refugee problem but to examine the problem in the light of current realities, with a view toward clarifying aspects that may affect its resolution today. Nor is the purpose to offer new or unique proposals for solution of the problem; there is no shortage of such proposals. However, none of the proposed solutions is viable outside the context of an overall resolution of the Arab-Israeli conflict. On the other hand, no credible resolution of the refugee problem can be achieved outside the context of regional economic and social development, for during the past 45 years the refugee problem has become part of the overall issue of regional development. Furthermore, any discussion of regional development must take into consideration the Palestine refugee issue.

Finally, let me address a terminology issue. The reader will no doubt notice that I use the term "Palestine refugee" rather than "Palestinian refugee." I chose the former term simply to conform to the practice of UNRWA, the agency charged with refugee care, whose full name is the United Nations Relief and Works Agency for Palestine Refugees in the Near East. No political or other nuances were intended.

Palestinians, Refugees,
and the Middle East Peace Process

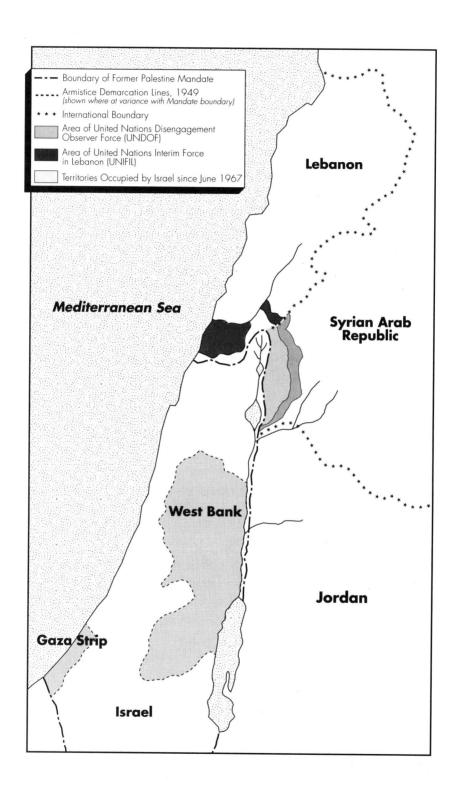

Boundary of Former Palestine Mandate

Armistice Demarcation Lines, 1949
(shown where at variance with Mandate boundary)

★ ★ ★ International Boundary

Area of United Nations Disengagement Observer Force (UNDOF)

Area of United Nations Interim Force in Lebanon (UNIFIL)

Territories Occupied by Israel since June 1967

Lebanon

Mediterranean Sea

Syrian Arab Republic

West Bank

Jordan

Gaza Strip

Israel

Introduction

Since 1948, the Palestine Arab refugee problem has been a focal point in the conflict between Israel and its Arab neighbors. During the first 20 years after the creation of Israel, many observers perceived the refugee problem as the most crucial issue; thus major attention was devoted to it in the expectation that resolution of this problem would be instrumental in ending the conflict. Western policymakers continue to regard resolution of the Arab-Israeli conflict as a major, if not the most important, prerequisite for achieving political and social stability in the Middle East, and many regard solution of the refugee problem as the key to peace between Israel and its Arab neighbors. This is not to imply that the region is not confronted with a host of other problems that create instability, or that within the context of the Arab-Israeli conflict there are not numerous other issues in dispute. However, the refugee issue cuts across the spectrum of problems, and the fate of the refugees is therefore related to such other complicated issues as regional economic and social development, the use of water resources, and political stability in several countries in the area.

◀ UNRWA area of operations. From *United Nations Relief and Works Agency for Palestine Refugees in the Near East, 1991/92* (UNRWA Public Information Office, 1992). According to UNRWA, this map "may not be considered as an authority on the delineation of international boundaries."

Background

Great Britain governed Palestine from 1917–18, when it was captured from the Ottoman Empire, until May 1948. British authority was given international recognition in 1922, when the League of Nations established a British mandate over Palestine.

The Palestine refugee problem began in 1947–48 as a result of the first Arab-Israeli war following the United Nations resolution to partition Palestine into an Arab state, a Jewish state, and an international enclave to include Jerusalem and its environs. Arab opposition to the partition resolution erupted into war between mandatory Palestine's Arab and Jewish inhabitants, a war that spread as the surrounding Arab countries attempted to defeat the newly established state of Israel following British departure from the country in 1948. During the course of the war more than 700,000 Palestinian Arabs fled to neighboring areas. Most went to Gaza, then under Egyptian occupation; to the West Bank, then part of the Hashemite Emirate of Transjordan (later the Kingdom of Jordan); to Syria; and to Lebanon.

Arab defeat in the first Arab-Israeli war led to nearly total disruption of the Palestine Arab community and its dispersal throughout the Middle East. The traditional organizations, establishments, and social structure of the community were shattered, most of its leaders were gone, and only a small remnant of the community remained in the area under Israeli control. Of the approximately 800,000 Arabs originally situated in the area that became Israel, only about 100,000 remained in their homes; they became Israeli citizens, an Arab minority in the Jewish state.

Since 1948 the refugee problem has been one of the most controversial in the Arab-Israeli conflict. The official Arab position has been that the refugees were driven from their homes by Jewish—later Israeli—forces. Israel and its supporters maintain that Israel was not responsible for the flight but that the refugees departed under instructions from their leaders or at the behest of neighboring Arab authorities, although recently several Israeli "revisionist" historians have raised the issue of Israel's shared accountability for the flight.

The issue of responsibility for the refugee flight affects the many ramifications of the problem, such as compensation, the "right of return," and resettlement or repatriation of the refugees; it cuts across most other aspects of the conflict and has been a major obstacle to its resolution since 1947–48.

After the 1967 Six Day War, attention shifted to the political aspects of the Palestine problem; there was growing emphasis on the question of creating a Palestine state in the Israeli-occupied West Bank and Gaza. Nevertheless, the refugee issue remained. The number of refugees increased constantly and their maintenance led to ever larger allocations of funds from the international community to the United Nations Relief and Works Agency for Palestine Refugees in the Near East (UNRWA), the UN agency charged with Palestine refugee care.

This refugee problem differs from others in several respects. It has persisted longer, some 45 years since the first Palestinian exodus in 1947–48. During this nearly half century, the United Nations has accepted responsibility for care and maintenance of the Palestine refugees, for which expenditures total some $4 billion. According to annual UNRWA reports, these expenditures have risen from $33.6 million a year when UNRWA became responsible for the refugees in 1950 to over $254.5 million in 1991. During this period, UNRWA has become one of the largest international organizations, employing some 19,000 people.

Since 1949, the Palestine refugee problem has appeared on the agenda at every session of the UN General Assembly, and it has been the subject of more resolutions than most other items discussed at the United Nations. Support for these resolutions is one area in which the Arab members of the United Nations vote as a bloc, and the appearance of the refugee issue on the annual agenda of the General Assembly underscores the importance that the Arab members and several other members of the Islamic Conference attach to the refugees. Indeed, the refugee problem has acquired a certain symbolism—the continued presence of the refugees symbolizes the continuation of the Arab-Israeli conflict. These factors have given the issue a political significance not acquired by other refugee problems of concern to the international community, some of them far larger in numbers and in the seriousness of their impact on the refugees involved.

In recent years, with attention focused on the question of a Palestine state or other political entity, less emphasis has been placed on the long-term prospects for resolving the refugee problem, although some observers believe that establishment of a Palestine state will automatically lead to substantial amelioration, if not total resolution, of the dilemma. The issue again acquired prominence as a result of the Gulf War during 1990 and at the Middle East peace conference convened in Madrid following the Gulf War.

During the Gulf War, the problem of refugees was intensified by the exodus from Kuwait of several hundred thousand Palestinians, many of them stateless. Unlike the several million other refugees resulting from the war, many Palestinians who either fled or were expelled from Kuwait had no country to which they could return. Jordan became their principal temporary host because the great majority had Jordanian travel documents. A smaller number carried Egyptian documents, but they were barred from entering Egypt or Gaza, which had formerly been under Egyptian occupation. During and after the Gulf War, there was a convergence of the Palestine refugee problem with the much larger problem of other refugees from Iraq, Kuwait, and other Gulf countries. However, most of the non-Palestinians were nationals of various Arab and Asian nations, including Egypt, Yemen, Pakistan, India, Bangladesh, and the Philippines. The non-Palestinians, too, encountered great economic hardship resulting from their sudden dislocation, but most of them did find homelands to which they could return and which were willing to accept them.

The refugee issue had not been scheduled on the agenda of the Middle East peace conference that convened in Madrid during October 1991; however, it emerged as one of the five important problems that the conference decided to deal with at a second multilateral phase of negotiations in Moscow during January 1992. In Moscow, the more than twenty nations participating in the multilateral discussions decided to convene a third multinational round of talks on these five issues during the spring of 1992. The issues were the environment, water, disarmament and security, economic development, and refugees. Thus the refugee issue again became a major, if not the central, focus of efforts to resolve the conflict between Israel and its neighbors.

Although the Palestine refugee problem is a critical factor in maintaining Middle East stability, it cannot be dealt with in isolation from other issues affecting regional stability, such as those designated in Moscow in January 1992. Settlement of the refugee issue must address problems such as the security of Israel, internal stability in the Arab host countries, and various aspects of international law dealing with refugees in general and specifically with matters such as compensation, the right of return, and human rights. The issue also is intimately related to the settlement of borders between Israel and its neighbors: Will a Palestine entity be independent, autonomous, linked with Jordan, or linked with Israel? International assistance to the refugees raises questions about the future of UNRWA and the type of assistance the refugees will receive in the future—whether the emphasis should be on continued education, vocational training, social welfare assistance, or development programs that could integrate the refugees within the region.

The refugee working group convened at Ottawa, Canada, in May 1992 did not restrict its proceedings to the Palestinians but was open to discussion of other refugee issues arising from the Arab-Israeli conflict, such as the problem of Jewish refugees from Arab countries and the problem of inhabitants of south Lebanon who had been victimized by conflict there between Israel and various Lebanese armed factions. By implication, these problems were linked. For example, many Israelis have linked compensation for Palestinian property left in Israel with compensation for property abandoned by Jewish refugees from Arab countries, including Iraq, Syria, Lebanon, and Egypt.

It is evident that the Palestine refugee question has to be part of both an interim and a final solution of the conflict because the interests of diaspora Palestinians, both refugees and others, are closely linked with the interests of Palestinians in the West Bank and Gaza. Failure of Palestinian negotiators to consider the concerns and interests of those outside the borders of the former Palestine would undermine the credibility of the peace process. Diaspora refugees would perceive neglect of their interests as betrayal, and this perception would stimulate further unrest in diaspora communities where there is already increasing disenchantment with the leadership, the governments of host countries, and the international community.

Current Status

Numbers

The definition of the term *Palestine refugees*, the refugees' status in host countries, and the conditions in which they live have changed over the years and often vary from country to country. These changes affect the refugees' own attitudes about their future and are relevant to prospects and plans of the various parties attempting to resolve the refugee problem. Today the term *Palestinian* usually refers to Arab inhabitants of mandatory Palestine or their descendants, about half of whom are classified by UNRWA as refugees. The refugees include a few thousand non-Arabs such as Armenians and others, mostly Christians, who lived in mandatory Palestine, and their descendants. (During the mandate all inhabitants of the country—Jews, Christians, Muslims, and others—were classified as Palestinians. With the establishment of Israel, Jewish Palestinians became identified as Israelis.)

Over the years, UNRWA has used different definitions of the term Palestine refugee. Originally, the definition was "a needy person, who, as a result of the war in Palestine, has lost his home and his means of livelihood." According to UNRWA's present definition,

A Palestine refugee is a person whose normal residence was Palestine for a minimum of two years preceding the conflict in 1948, and who, as a result of this conflict, lost both his home and his means of livelihood and took refuge in one of the countries where UNRWA provides relief. Refugees within this definition and the direct descendants of such refugees are eligible for Agency assistance if they are:

registered with UNRWA; living in the area of UNRWA operations; and in need.[1]

Note that the term refugee applies to those who left homes in Palestine *and their descendants.* Today the vast majority are descendants. Note also that UNRWA's definition of Palestine refugees is limited to those it has registered in the Arab host countries of Lebanon, the Syrian Arab Republic, and Jordan, as well as in the Israeli-occupied West Bank and Gaza.

The original UNRWA definition included some 17,000 Jews who had lived in areas of Palestine taken over by Arab forces during the 1948 war and about 50,000 Arabs living within Israel's 1949 armistice frontiers. However, Israel quickly took responsibility for these individuals, and by 1950 they were removed from the UNRWA rolls, leaving only Palestinian Arabs and a few hundred non-Arab Christian Palestinians outside Israel in the refugee category.[2]

The number of original Palestine refugees is based on estimates rather than an accurate count undertaken at the time of their departure from Palestine. The United Nations estimated in 1949 that more than 700,000 of Palestine's 1948 Arab population could be classified as refugees. During UNRWA's first year of operations, 940,000 refugees were registered, but that number was reduced by 1951, when individuals who did not fit the UNRWA definition were removed from the rolls.[3] Since then UNRWA has periodically attempted to rectify its lists, but because refugees are suspicious of attempts to gather information about them, these efforts have not been very successful.

UNRWA acknowledges that it cannot carry out a proper census: "The number of registered refugees [actually] present in the area of operations is almost certainly less than that recorded."[4] UNRWA's registration figures and its budget are based on the number of persons receiving its services. The organization maintains lists of persons who are registered as refugees and separate lists of those who qualify for its various services, such as rations, financial support, infant care, health care, and social welfare.[5] For example, in 1990 there were 357,000 refugees participating in education and training programs, 2 million eligible for health care, and 142,000 eligible for "special hardship" assistance.[6]

As of December 1992, the total number of refugees registered with UNRWA was 2.7 million (table 1). Refugees thus constitute about half of the more than 5 million people identified as Palestinians.[7]

The overall population growth rate of Palestinians, including refugees, is one of the highest in the world, more than 3 percent a year. The last estimate of the number of Palestinian Arabs in mandatory Palestine prior to their exodus during the first Arab-Israeli war in 1947–49 was about 1,380,000. Since then, the number has increased by more than 400 percent; the U.S. Census Bureau estimates that the total will reach more than 9 million by the year 2010, an increase of almost 700 percent within a 60-year period (table 2).[8]

A second major exodus of Palestinians occurred in the three months following the June 1967 war, when over 300,000 Palestinians left the West Bank and the Golan area. Some 120,000 of these were second-time refugees who had spent the 20 years before 1967 in refugee camps under Jordanian or Syrian jurisdiction in the West Bank or the Golan area. In addition to the second-time refugees, there were several thousand other individuals displaced from their homes for whom UNRWA took responsibility.[9]

Although the Palestinian population is widely dispersed throughout the Middle East, not all of those living beyond the borders of mandatory Palestine are classified as refugees, even though several million no longer live in their original homes or country of origin. A comparison of UNRWA refugee figures and U.S. Census Bureau estimates of the total number of Palestinians shows that of Jordan's more than 1.5 million Palestinians, about 1 million are refugees. Refugees constitute about 85 to 90 percent of the Palestinians in Lebanon, over 90 percent of those in Syria, over 40 percent of those in the West Bank, and two-thirds of those in the Gaza region. There are no "official" refugees among the Arab citizens of Israel.

Estimates of the total number of Palestinians vary. There has not yet been a reliable census. The problem is difficult because Palestinians are scattered in many countries of the Middle East, with several tens of thousands in Europe and the Americas as well. An estimate by the U.S. Census Bureau put the total number of Palestinians in the Middle East in 1990 at over 5.25 million. Palestine

Table 1. UNRWA General Information Sheet Concerning Refugees Under Its Jurisdiction.

	Lebanon	Syrian Arab Rep.	Jordan	Gaza	West Bank	Head-quarters	Total/Avg.
Country area (sq. km)	10,432	185,180	91,860	360	5,500		293,352
Country population (CP)	3,200,000	12,600,000	3,700,000	775,000	1,200,000		21,475,000
Registered refugees (RR)	324,219	306,042	1,042,123	582,863	472,573		2,727,820
RR average annual growth (%)	2.9	3.0	3.6	4.7	5.0		3.7
RR as % of CP	10.1	2.4	28.2	75.2	39.4		12.7
RR as % of total RR	11.9	11.2	38.2	21.4	17.3		100.0
Existing camps	12	10	10	8	19		59
RR in camps (RRCs)	169,321	88,924	237,677	320,467	124,307		904,696
RRCs as % of RR	52.2	29.1	22.8	55.0	26.3		34.5
Schools	76	111	201	153	100		641
Pupils (1992/93 enrollment)	33,172	60,216	152,350	104,709	42,310		392,757
Female pupils (%)	49.7	48.3	48.8	47.9	54.9		49.2
Training centres	1	1	2	1	3		8
Vocational training places	644	776	1,192	728	1,156		4,496
Teacher training places	0	0	225	0	420		645
In-service teacher training	213	202	281	225	154		1,075
University scholarships (1992/93)	42	156	187	203	158		746
Health centres/units	26	21	20	17	34		118
Dental clinics	14	8	16	8	15		61
Laboratories	12	11	17	7	17		64
Annual patient visits	787,408	830,924	1,525,070	2,013,692	930,352		6,087,446
Indoor water supply in camps (%)	89	75	92	100	98		92

Sewered shelters in camps (%)	56	85	45	27	31		47
Special hardship cases (SHCs)	37,094	20,141	28,387	54,914	30,265		170,801
SHCs as % of RR	11.4	6.6	2.7	9.4	6.4		6.3
Women's programme centres	10	12	20	14	11		67
Community rehab. centres (CRCs)	1	2	5	2	6		16
Self-support projects	159	51	171	107	53		541
Income-generation loans (no.)	2	0	14	70	24		110
Income-generation loans ($)	100,000	0	124,752	1,575,646	712,369		2,512,767
Area staff (posts)	2,492	2,707	6,102	4,868	3,119	320	19,608
International staff (posts)	8	7	8	30	33	101	187
Regular budget (GF), 1993 ($000)							
Education	12,118	20,778	39,619	35,393	21,557	17,768	147,233
Health	7,369	6,402	9,614	12,693	11,956	4,572	52,606
Relief and social services	6,658	3,349	5,885	8,924	5,244	1,923	31,983
Operational services	2,586	3,529	2,786	3,216	4,845	6,389	23,351
Common services	2,809	2,479	3,279	3,670	4,244	25,531	42,012
Total	31,540	36,537	61,183	63,896	47,846	56,183	297,185
EMLOT budget, 1993 ($000)	1,954	85	0	8,988	7,874	860	19,761
Unemployment % (est.)	40	10	20	34-40	30-40		28
Illiteracy %: 15 years+ (est.)	M12,F27	M22,F49	M11,F30	M10,F27	M11,F30		M12,F31
Infant mortality/1,000 (est.)	40	40	40	40	40		40

Notes: EMLOT stands for Extraordinary Measures in Lebanon and the Occupied Territory. M = male, F = female. All figures as of December 1992. All references are to agency installations.

Source: Programme Planning and Evaluation Office, UNRWA, January 1993.

Table 2. Projected Numbers of Palestinians (Refugees and Nonrefugees) in Sixteen Mideast Countries/Areas, 1990–2010.

Country/Area	1990	1995	2000	2005	2010
Algeria	4,661	5,119	5,571	6,022	6,465
Bahrain	2,174	2,381	2,598	2,851	3,110
Egypt	40,063	44,016	47,945	51,952	56,000
Gaza Strip	622,016	726,832	837,699	949,795	1,060,485
Iraq	29,922	35,876	42,277	49,639	58,245
Israel	686,895	800,755	919,453	1,039,314	1,160,371
Jordan	1,524,179	1,870,342	2,255,908	2,664,867	3,092,149
Kuwait	311,742	355,759	403,078	448,241	488,234
Lebanon	331,757	392,315	463,067	533,492	603,663
Libya	27,530	32,033	37,014	41,945	46,595
Oman	6,636	7,352	8,169	8,996	9,713
Qatar	30,995	33,941	37,058	40,714	44,471
Saudi Arabia	205,840	247,820	299,136	361,383	434,485
Syria	301,744	357,881	410,599	460,188	514,743
United Arab Emirates	47,374	52,186	57,619	63,195	68,149
West Bank	1,075,531	1,227,545	1,383,415	1,541,996	1,705,107
Total	5,249,059	6,192,153	7,210,606	8,264,590	9,351,985

Notes: Figures for Israel exclude urban East Jerusalem and the Golan Heights; figures for the West Bank include urban East Jerusalem.

Source: U.S. Bureau of the Census, Center for International Research, *Palestinian Projections for 16 Countries/Areas of the World 1990 to 2010* (Washington, D.C., March 1991, mimeographed).

Liberation Organization (PLO) sources give a figure of 5.7 million. Numbers and percentages used in this volume are based primarily on estimates of the U.S. Census Bureau and UNRWA.

The largest concentration of Palestinians in 1990 lived under Israeli jurisdiction, with 1,076,000 in the West Bank (of whom 150,000 lived in East Jerusalem), 622,000 in the Gaza Strip, and 687,000 Palestinian Arab citizens of Israel.[10] Thus, about half of those identified as Palestinians live in Israel and the territories it occupied during the 1967 Six Day War. Other large concentrations of Palestinians are located in Jordan (1,500,000 prior to the influx from Kuwait), Lebanon (332,000), Kuwait (312,000 before the Gulf War), Syria (302,000), and Saudi Arabia (206,000). Several tens of

Table 3. Projected Percentages of Palestinians (Refugees and Nonrefugees) in the Total Population of Sixteen Mideast Countries/Areas, 1990–2010.

Country/Area	1990	1995	2000	2005	2010
Algeria	.01	.01	.01	.01	.01
Bahrain	0.4	0.4	0.4	0.4	0.4
Egypt	0.1	0.1	0.1	0.1	0.1
Gaza Strip	100.0	100.0	100.0	100.0	100.0
Iraq	0.2	0.2	0.2	0.2	0.2
Israel	15.5	16.2	17.3	18.2	19.0
Jordan	46.6	46.5	46.2	45.8	45.4
Kuwait	37.1	34.7	32.4	29.8	27.0
Lebanon	9.9	10.8	11.4	11.8	12.2
Libya	0.7	0.7	0.7	0.7	0.7
Oman	0.4	0.4	0.4	0.4	0.3
Qatar	6.3	5.4	5.0	4.8	4.7
Saudi Arabia	1.2	1.2	1.2	1.2	1.3
Syria	2.4	2.3	2.2	2.1	2.0
United Arab Emirates	2.1	1.8	1.6	1.5	1.4
West Bank	100.0	100.0	100.0	100.0	100.0

Source: U.S. Bureau of the Census, Center for International Research, *Palestinian Projections for 16 Countries/Areas of the World 1990 to 2010* (Washington, D.C., March 1991, mimeographed).

thousands are located in a dozen other Arab countries as well (see table 2).[11]

In 1990, Palestinians constituted the largest percentages of the total population in Jordan (47 percent), prewar Kuwait (37), Israel within its pre-1967 frontiers (16), Lebanon (10), and Qatar (6). In other countries with more than 100,000 Palestinians, such as Syria and Saudi Arabia, they were less than 3 percent of the total population (table 3).[12]

Characteristics

About 98 percent of the current refugees either are Palestinian nationals or are descendants of Palestinian nationals. The other 2 percent lived in Palestine but were not nationals of the country when the mandate ended. This 2 percent includes Lebanese, Syrians, Egyptians, Greeks, Sudanese, Turks, Tunisians, Russians, and more

Table 4. Life Expectancy at Birth and Fertility Indicators for Palestinians, 1967–1992.

	1967/ 1972	1972/ 1977	1977/ 1982	1982/ 1987	1987/ 1992
Fertility rate, by age group[a]					
15–19	108	98	94	92	89
20–24	389	353	339	330	321
25–29	449	406	391	380	370
30–34	362	328	315	306	298
35–39	266	241	232	225	219
40–44	96	87	84	82	79
45–49	29	26	25	25	24
Gross fertility rate[b]	8.5	7.7	7.4	7.2	7.0
Life expectancy at birth	53	56	58	61	63

[a] Number of births per 1,000 women.
[b] Number of births per woman.
Source: *Population Bulletin of ESCWA* (UN Economic and Social Commission for West Asia) no. 27 (Baghdad, December 1985).

than twenty other nationalities. Today nearly 40 percent of the refugees hold or are eligible for Jordanian passports. Most of the original refugees were small landowners, farmworkers, or laborers. Today, the average age of refugees registered with UNRWA is 28.1 years; about one-third are age 15 or younger. More than 96 percent are Muslims. Three-fourths or more of the 450,000 refugee families are headed by men. The average number of children per family is 3.7; the largest families are those in Jordan, with an average of 5.6 children.[13] As Palestinians have acquired more education, vocational skills, and upward mobility, there has been a decline in the fertility rate and an increase in life expectancy (table 4).

Living Conditions

Originally, most refugees were accommodated in camps established by the UN Relief for Palestine Refugees (UNRPR); after 1950, UNRWA provided services to the camps, although it did not administer them. Control of the camps varied; in some areas they were run by the refugees, in others by host government agencies. However, by the 1950s and 1960s many refugees found homes elsewhere, although they continued to receive a wide variety of UNRWA services, including health care, education, vocational training, social welfare assistance, and food rations. By the end of 1992 only a third of the UNRWA refugees continued to live in camps. The percentage of refugees living in camps ranged from 23 percent in Jordan to 55 percent in the Gaza Strip. There were a total of 59 camps: 19 in the West Bank, 12 in Lebanon, 10 in Jordan, 10 in Syria, and 8 in the Gaza Strip (see table 1).

When UNRWA took over from UNRPR in 1950, most of its funds were used to provide basic necessities, mainly food and shelter. However, when many refugees found employment and were able to provide their own basic needs, expenditures shifted to improving living standards and quality of life. Most UNRWA resources are used for education, and more than half the UNRWA staff of about 19,000 is involved in education. UNRWA's clinics and medical facilities, nutritional assistance, basic sanitation work, and education programs have provided those under its care with one of the best networks of relatively sophisticated social and educational services in the Arab countries of the Middle East.

The refugees who reside in the 59 camps serviced by UNRWA are entitled to receive all services. Other UNRWA-registered refugees may receive some or all services depending on need, as determined by family size, income, and similar qualifications. Many men have left the camps to find employment elsewhere, either within the host country or abroad. They usually send back remittances to their families, who also continue to receive the range of UNRWA services mentioned above.

During the oil boom of the 1970s and the resulting rapid expansion and development of the Gulf region, many from the camps found work in the Gulf. Some took their families with them; others left behind wives and children. As the economy of the Gulf began to cool off in the 1980s, many Palestinians returned to their former host countries, since they could not go back to their ancestral homes in Israel or the Occupied Territories. A similar situation prevailed following the 1990 Gulf War, when hundreds of thousands fled or were forced to leave Kuwait, Iraq, Saudi Arabia, and surrounding countries.

Following the invasion of Kuwait, UNRWA provided emergency assistance to several hundred thousand Palestinians who arrived in Jordan. UNRWA's responsibilities also were increased as a result of the curfew imposed by Israel on the West Bank and Gaza, which prevented Palestinians from leaving their homes for lengthy periods. These restrictions necessitated emergency food distributions to thousands in the Occupied Territories who were not on the refugee rolls. Emergency assistance was necessary because nearly half of the West Bank and Gaza Palestinian working population was prevented from entering Israel, where they had been employed before the war. UNRWA emergency assistance was again required in 1993, when Israel closed its borders to most Palestinian workers from Gaza and the West Bank following terrorist attacks on Jewish civilians.

As noted above, not all Palestinians in the Middle East are refugees. Some Palestinians have achieved the highest economic, political, and social status, even though they live in exile. Many have served as cabinet members, ambassadors, and heads of important government agencies in Jordan, Syria, Kuwait, and Saudi Arabia. A few Palestinian businessmen have become multimillionaires through a variety of enterprises, including banking, construction, trade, and commerce. The president of the Arab world's largest private bank is a Palestinian, as are the owners of the region's leading private international construction company. The owner of the Ritz-Carlton hotels in New York and Washington is a Palestinian. A Palestinian was the architect of Kuwait's highly profitable overseas investments.[14]

Many Palestinians in the upper middle and middle class have achieved renown as physicians, scientists, journalists, and academics. Thousands from the middle class have provided essential skills at middle levels of government and as teachers and technicians in Jordan and the Gulf states. At the bottom of the social scale, Palestinians in Lebanon, Syria, and Jordan have provided unskilled labor during labor shortages when the economies of these countries were expanding rapidly (table 5).

Table 5. Occupational Distribution of Palestinian Men in Selected Countries and Regions.

Country or Region of Residence	Percentage in Occupational Categories by Descending Status						
	Prof./Techn.	Admin./Manager	Sales/Clerical	Indus./Commercial	Trans./Util.	Agric./Serv. (pers.)	Fish./Mining
Saudi Arabia (1974)	51.5	2.9	6.0	3.2	28.9	3.3	4.3
Jordanians	63.0	3.1	6.1	3.1	20.1	1.9	2.1
Palestinians	36.9	2.6	5.7	3.3	39.3	5.0	7.1
Kuwait (1975)	20.8	1.3	17.8	8.6	41.1	8.4	2.1
Jordan East Bank (1975 Amman)	9.7		7.0	11.8	45.4	11.2	14.5
Syria (1970)	10.8	0.7	8.2	8.9	57.0	6.6	7.9
Israel (1980)	7.8		2.2	5.9	58.8	10.0	15.0
West Bank (1980)	6.1	0.9	2.7	12.0	53.4	7.3	17.6
Gaza (1980)	4.3	0.8	2.3	11.7	53.8	8.6	18.5
Lebanon camps (1971)	3.7		1.4	15.3	46.1	8.9	24.7

Sources: Data are from Janet Abu-Lughod, "Demographic Characteristics of the Palestinian Population," annex 1, pt. 2, of *Palestine Open University Feasibility Study* (Paris: UNESCO, 1980), 61; *Statistical Abstract of Israel* no. 32 (1981), tables XVII/21, XII/17; *Palestine Statistical Abstract* (Damascus: Palestine National Fund, 1980).

Many refugees who have risen to middle-class status wish to retain their official UNRWA cards as the only documentation of their Palestinian origin and as an expression of political solidarity with the larger Palestinian community. Many who no longer require UNRWA assistance keep their documentation in the hope that those classified as refugees might one day receive compensation. In addition to these "official" refugees, there are thousands of individuals who never registered with UNRWA for a variety of reasons, who were never integrated into the mainstream of diaspora life, and who continue to live an impoverished existence.

The level of education and literacy among Palestinians is one of the highest in the Middle East. A survey of Palestinians from the West Bank and Gaza Strip living in the surrounding countries showed that more than a fifth were secondary school or university graduates and that illiterates were relatively few. Among university graduates, more than half specialized in the humanities, one-fifth in engineering, about one-tenth in medicine, and the balance in pure sciences. A report by the UN Economic and Social Commission for West Asia (ESCWA) in 1982 showed that the average number of years of schooling among Jordanian Palestinians in the Gulf ranged from seven in Kuwait to ten in the United Arab Emirates.[15]

A survey of occupations and professions among Palestinians in Kuwait undertaken by ESCWA during 1975 showed that

> They were engaged in scientific and technical occupations requiring post-graduate qualifications and high standards of technical skills respectively. They constituted 28 percent of all engineers, 34 percent of surveyors and draftsmen, 37 percent of all doctors and pharmacists, 25 percent of the nursing staff, 38 percent of all economists and accountants, 30 percent of the teaching staff, 23 percent of production supervisors and foremen, 20 percent of carpenters, 25 percent of blacksmiths and precision instrument manufacturers, 25 percent of electricians, 27 percent of sanitation equipment workers, and 26 percent of transport equipment operators.[16]

Palestinians of all social and economic origins and all political persuasions agree on the necessity of high-quality education for their youth. This is perhaps the highest priority of every Palestinian family;

it is seen as the key to the future, the path out of refugee camps and the lowly status of a permanent underclass throughout the Arab east. Even among the poorest refugee camp families with six, eight, or ten children, it is not unusual to find several individuals who are high school or university graduates or have technical school certificates.

As young Palestinians graduated from UNRWA schools, they sought upward mobility through lower level clerical and administrative jobs. This new class of subordinate white-collar workers (*muwazzafeen*) found a measure of security and stable income in such work, which raised them from the working class to the lower middle class. Few Palestinians became industrial workers; there was almost no Palestinian industrial development in the host countries because industry was the preserve of the native bourgeoisie and workforce.

Like diaspora Jews, the Palestinians produced in their diaspora or *ghourba* a much higher percentage of literate, technically trained, highly skilled workers than the level prevailing in the Arab host countries. Since 1948, a Palestinian bourgeoisie has arisen that is "remarkably dynamic, effective, audacious, and successful" in the host countries where Palestinians have ascended and become prominent "in the various realms of cultural production . . . [and achieved] superiority in such fields as trade, finance, banking, industry, and entrepreneurship in general."[17]

However, the expected rewards of high-level education are often not forthcoming, and this leads to great frustration, resentment of prevailing political establishments, and frequent radicalization of youth in their teens and early twenties. Many of those who were among the better educated went to the Gulf states or Saudi Arabia in the 1960s and 1970s. But when the oil boom ended and the producing states began to train their own professionals, technicians, and clerks, opportunities for Palestinians declined. The movement of the Palestinian labor force began to reverse as Palestinians returned from the Gulf, many to the refugee camps they had left a decade or more earlier.

Some now argue that too many Palestinians are overeducated and are no longer willing or able to do unskilled labor or jobs at the bottom of the economic scale. This situation was greatly exacerbated by the Gulf War, when not only Kuwait but other Gulf states deported tens of thousands of Palestinians who were perceived as having obtained too much economic and political influence. Among the approximately 300,000 Palestinians returning from Kuwait to Jordan and the 30,000 to 40,000 who came back to the Occupied Territories, many were highly skilled workers or professionals (no accurate census has been taken of the number who returned, but comments made during interviews by UNRWA, Jordanian, and Israeli officials support this estimate).

Most Palestinians, both those in camps and others, live in urban areas, concentrated in their own neighborhoods. Thus, many of the refugee camps have evolved over the past four decades into extensions of large cities such as Beirut, Damascus, and Amman. With over 65,000 inhabitants, Bakaa camp on the outskirts of Amman is the largest center of refugee concentration in the region. Many Bakaa residents have part-time or temporary jobs in the capital or in adjoining agricultural and commercial enterprises. They work as drivers, government clerks, health workers, bank employees, and the like. The camp has been transformed into a large refugee city with its own market center and a wide range of services such as small stores, auto repair shops, and barber shops. The camp also contains an extensive system of UNRWA services, including schools, clinics, and welfare centers of various types that provide special education and assistance for infants and the aged.

Budgets to support the UNRWA education and welfare systems have not increased in proportion to need. Population growth has put great strain on facilities available to refugees, a strain evident in the extreme overcrowding of classrooms, the long lines at clinics, and the spartan buildings that house these services. Although the dedication of teachers, physicians, and health workers is high, the time they are able to spend with each individual declines year by year. When a physician can afford to spend not more than two or three minutes per patient, the quality of care must inevitably decline. When teachers must handle classes of over forty students, sometimes two per desk, in antiquated rooms, the quality of education suffers.

Although the outward appearance of the camps has not changed greatly in the last decade or so, the problem of overcrowding is becoming acute. Most camp areas have not been extended, but tens of thousands of new inhabitants have been added to the original cramped enclosures. The situation has been particularly serious in the Gaza and West Bank refugee camps during the Intifada, the Palestine Arab uprising that began in December 1987 in the Occupied Territories; since that time the Israeli military has periodically imposed lengthy curfews, confining large families to small spaces for days and weeks at a time.

Space in the camps is allotted per family, regardless of family size. Families with half a dozen or more children must improvise expanded living arrangements in a very limited space. As the population increases, camp residents add rooms on top of the original structures—simple one-room cement enclosures—or in spaces that were intended as small courtyards, or they subdivide the original space into more but smaller rooms.

Since the early days of UNRWA, most refugees have found ways to tap into electricity and water systems. With encouragement from UNRWA, once-muddy alleyways meandering through camps are now being paved; UNRWA provides materials and camp residents do the work. From a distance, the camps appear to be typical Middle Eastern villages; in cities where several camps are located, they become adjuncts to surrounding urban slums. An important difference between traditional village life and life in the camps is that Palestinians registered with UNRWA are provided with a variety of services and facilities usually unavailable to the impoverished nonrefugee.

Development of Political Identity

A major difference in outlook between Palestinians in the camps and those outside is the extent to which camp residents are submerged in Palestinian consciousness. Few camp residents in the East Bank would identify themselves as Jordanian. They remain Palestinian despite their Jordanian passports or identity cards. Children in camps are socialized almost from infancy to regard themselves as Palestinians, not as Jordanians, Syrians, Lebanese, Egyptians, or Israelis.

Although UNRWA school systems use the official curricula of the host countries, Palestinian teachers and school administrators foster a strong Palestinian national identity. Even though the children, and in many cases their parents, have never seen Palestine, they believe that Palestine is their homeland. Palestinian identity is reinforced by school songs, maps and slogans on school walls, and the red, green, white, and black Palestinian flag atop camp buildings. When asked, "Where are you from?" children still reply with the name of the city, town, or village of their Palestinian origin. Few camp residents have been integrated into the mainstream of life in Amman, Damascus, or Beirut. This situation leads to more militant political attitudes among those in the camps than among those who have been integrated into the mainstream in the host countries.

Until recently, most political leadership in the Palestinian community came from the middle- and upper-middle-class elite—professionals such as teachers, lawyers, and physicians. Since the Intifada, many young men from the refugee camps have ascended to leadership, and camp voices have become louder. Indeed, the first large-scale demonstrations of the Intifada began in the refugee camps of Gaza and the West Bank. The Occupied Territories started a pattern of change in leadership observed in Jordan as well.

As the date of the original exodus from Palestine reaches the half-century mark, a third and fourth generation of Palestinians and refugees who never saw Palestine are reaching maturity. Nevertheless, Palestinian consciousness remains strong. Palestinians have maintained themselves as a distinctive group, both within the Occupied Territories and in the diaspora. Furthermore, those among whom they live—either as a majority, in Jordan, the West Bank, and Gaza, or as a minority, in Lebanon, Syria, Kuwait, and elsewhere in the Middle East—also perceive them as a distinctive group.

Palestinians' social relations and employment contacts are largely with other Palestinians. In their daily lives, Palestinians are constantly reminded of their identity, both by their own community and by the non-Palestinian authorities under whose jurisdiction they must live.

According to Palestinians and those who work with them, even in the two countries where Palestinians have become citizens, Israel and Jordan, they are perceived by the authorities as less than full-fledged members of the community because they continue to be mistrusted. In all countries where there are large concentrations of Palestinians, they are the target of official repression that varies in its intensity from place to place. Although all Arab countries have espoused the Palestinian cause as a principal theme in the rhetoric of pan-Arab nationalism, Palestinians, especially those in the refugee camps, are subjected to periodic security investigations and persistent police surveillance.

As a result of this situation, a form of "Palestinian Zionism" has emerged. Sadik Al-Azm, a professor at Damascus University, has described the similarities between Palestinian and Jewish Zionism.[18] These include the predominantly urban character of both communities and the urban nature of their activities. One of the major socioeconomic results of the collapse of Palestinian society in 1947–48 was its "depeasantization," the change in occupational distribution and social organization from a mostly agricultural peasant community to an urban lumpenproletariat bereft of the farm land that had been its economic base. An estimated two-thirds of the refugees were of peasant origin; few, however, found employment in agriculture. Most in the camps worked as unskilled casual laborers at wages below those prevailing for such work in the host countries. Initially their subsistence was made possible by assistance, especially food rations from UNRWA.

Relations between Palestinians and the host populations have often been characterized by tension and oppression. In nearly every country where Palestinians live concentrated in large numbers, this tension has produced friction that at one time or another has degenerated into physical altercations among Palestinians, host authorities, and local populations. Like most diaspora Jews, the Palestinians have rejected assimilation or absorption into larger national movements. In most host countries, they are often perceived as the cause of unrest and instability and are therefore denied integration into the mainstream of society.

After the Arab defeat in the 1948 war and Palestinian dispersion in the countries surrounding Israel, most Palestinian political leaders became discredited. Although the Palestinian masses grew dispirited, a minority continued their political activity, often by establishing relationships with opposition groups in the host countries. Such factions as the Arab Nationalist Movement, the Syrian Social Nationalist Movement, the Ba'ath Party, the Communists, and the Muslim Brothers were particularly successful in recruiting younger Palestinians.

Egyptian president Gamal Abd al-Nasser's apparent successes during the late 1950s and 1960s and his personal charisma appealed to the Palestinians as well as to Arabs generally throughout the region. Many regarded him almost as a messiah who would redeem Palestine and make it possible for Palestinians to return to their homes. Before the 1967 defeat, pictures of Nasser adorned Palestinian and other Arab homes throughout the region. The euphoria of Nasserism continued to block alternative affiliations in the camps until 1967; "perhaps the real break came with Nasser's acceptance of the Rogers Plan in the summer of 1970."[19]

Remnants of the old-guard Palestinian leadership were active in the camps in the 1960s and early 1970s; Haj Amin al-Husseini, the former mufti of Jerusalem, had followers among the older generation, and his representatives attempted to extend their control through heads of families and *hamula* (extended family) networks. This effort was facilitated by the fact that the camps were still organized according to traditional village social structure.

By the early 1960s, distinctive Palestinian organizations began to organize on paramilitary lines with the purpose of engaging Israel in armed struggle. The most important of these organizations was Fatah, although the PLO, established during a summit of Arab leaders in 1964, was more visible. Initially, the PLO was perceived by nationalist militants as a tool of the Arab regimes to control the Palestinians.

With the defeat of Egypt, Syria, and Jordan during the June 1967 war, a defeat that had a far greater impact on Arab society than the events of 1948, Palestinians became increasingly disenchanted with the nationalist organizations and with the leaders to whom they had pledged their loyalty, such as Nasser.

Following the June 1967 war, several new Palestinian organizations were established, most with the objective of "liberating" Palestine through armed struggle. Increasingly, attention shifted from the Palestine Arab refugee problem to the political issue of establishing a Palestinian state. Initially, nearly all factions focused on armed struggle, believing that guerrilla warfare could somehow undermine the Jewish state. At first, none of these groups was willing to accept a political compromise that envisaged the continued existence of Israel. Not until the 1970s did one or two leftist factions begin to move toward a two-state solution.

By 1968, the PLO had become the organization generally accepted as the representative of the Palestinians; it included several factions that disagreed among themselves about Palestinian relationships with the Jewish people, Zionism, and the state of Israel. By far the largest of these groups was Fatah, led by Yasir Arafat; Arafat was also elected president of the PLO. However, political differences among the diverse factions prevented any real compromise until the Intifada erupted in December 1987.

The PLO was organized like a government in exile, and by the 1970s it had received diplomatic status from all Arab states and several dozen other countries; it was also given observer status in the principal organs of the UN. In addition to its political, diplomatic, and paramilitary activities, the PLO organized an extensive network of economic and social functions. This infrastructure included a complex of health care, welfare, cultural, educational, and recreational institutions as well as several businesses that generated hundreds of millions of dollars. Participants in these activities were organized in a number of unions, including the General Union of Palestinian Women and unions for workers, engineers, writers, and students. It was these diverse organizations, the central institutions of the PLO, and the Palestine National Council (PNC) that transformed the Palestinians, especially the refugees, into a people with a distinctive Palestinian voice.

The Intifada began a new phase in the development of Palestinian nationalism. It shifted the focus of attention and the center of decision making from leaders in the diaspora, such as Arafat and the PLO executive, to the Israeli-occupied West Bank and Gaza. The Intifada represented a new generation and a new leadership cadre—younger, unknown Palestinians rather than the traditional notables from the middle- and upper-middle-class professional elite. Many formerly unknown individuals, both men and women, from refugee camps and the working class were in the vanguard of the uprising.

Initially the Intifada galvanized the whole Palestinian community within the Occupied Territories. It overcame many of the divisions in Palestinian society, such as those between rural villages and the towns, between refugee-camp inhabitants and nonrefugees, and between Muslims and Christians. Women were more active than before in political decision making and in resistance activities.

Although Muslim fundamentalists had been among the first to demonstrate against the occupation, the newly established Hamas (the Islamic Resistance Movement, known by its Arabic acronym) did not participate in the Unified National Leadership of the Uprising (UNLU), an underground organization representing Fatah, the Popular Front for the Liberation of Palestine, the Democratic Popular Front, and the Palestine Communists. Hamas and Islamic Jihad issued their own leaflets and directives against the occupation. Whereas the UNLU, representing several factions affiliated with the PLO, called for establishment of an independent Palestinian state in the West Bank and Gaza to coexist with Israel, the militant fundamentalists opposed any compromise based on a two-state solution. They called for establishment of an Islamic state in all of Palestine. At first the fundamentalists either cooperated with or at least refrained from outright opposition to the UNLU. However, tensions began to develop among Hamas, Islamic Jihad, and the secular leaders of the uprising, many of them Christians. These tensions led to outright confrontation, often exploding into internecine violence. Economic conditions deteriorated and unemployment increased in the Occupied Territories, and the peace negotiations following the Madrid conference in 1991 dragged on; there was little indication that the objectives of the uprising would soon be achieved, and many Palestinians became disenchanted with the moderate tactics of the UNLU. Increasing numbers of restless inhabitants in the territories turned to the fundamentalists for direction and solace. Palestinians' sympathy toward Hamas was enhanced in December 1992, when the Israeli government expelled more than 400 Palestinians to Lebanon after accusing them of being responsible for terrorist activities. The deportations aroused the ire of nearly all Palestinians and the sympathy of Arab governments, many of which were themselves threatened by Islamic fundamentalist movements. The incident led to a special meeting of the Arab League, which called for a return of the expellees to Israel; even Israeli Arab leaders called on their government to rescind the deportation orders. More significant was that the expulsions led to an attempt to reconcile differences between the PLO leadership and Hamas, which was offered 18 seats in the 483-member PNC.

Another manifestation of impatience with the UNLU was the outbreak of vigilantism in the Palestinian community; small bands of youths took the law into their own hands seeking to punish "traitors" or "collaborators" among Palestinians suspected of being informers for or agents of Israeli intelligence. Black-hooded gangs with names like "Black Eagles" assassinated several hundred fellow Palestinians, whom they accused of disloyalty or of violating community social or moral norms. By the end of 1992 the number of Palestinians killed by these "superpatriots" was nearly half the total killed by the Israeli military during the first five years of the uprising.

Whereas the Intifada put pressure on parties in the Arab-Israeli conflict to reopen the political question of a Palestine state, it was the Gulf War and its aftermath that reopened the refugee issue. The war underscored the urgent need for Israel and its Arab neighbors to reach a peace settlement and accelerated the process initiated by the United States in 1988–89. Prior to this initiative, there had been little discussion of the many significant aspects of the refugee dilemma—problems such as refugee compensation, repatriation or resettlement, and development of projects for economic absorption of the refugees—since the mission of President John Kennedy's special representative to the Middle East, Joseph Johnson, in the early 1960s.

Although the Intifada and the Gulf War helped bring about the Madrid Middle East conference in 1991, little was accomplished in nearly two years of bilateral negotiations between Israel and Syria, Lebanon, Jordan, and the Palestinians and several rounds of multilateral parleys. In an effort to overcome the apparent stalemate, secret talks were arranged in Norway in 1993 between Israel's Labor government and the PLO. These discussions led to agreements between Israel and the PLO for mutual recognition and plans for Palestinian self-rule in Gaza and the West Bank town of Jericho. The agreements were notable in that they were the first official recognition by Israel of the PLO, an organization that all previous Israeli governments had labeled as "terrorist" and had shunned, and whose activities had been banned in the Occupied Territories. In effect, the September 1993 agreements were tantamount to Israeli recognition of Palestinian political identity. (For more on the agreement, see page 45.)

Recent Palestinian Perspectives

Observers who have spent lengthy periods of time with Palestinians, those who work among Palestinians, and leaders representing various Palestinian perspectives report recent attitudinal patterns that appear to be common among both refugees and nonrefugees.

Saddam Hussein's defeat in the Gulf War and the divisiveness the war created among Arab leaders; the collapse of the Soviet Union and evaporation of Moscow's support for Arab causes; the emergence of the United States (which is perceived as Israel's ally) as the only superpower; growing disillusionment with the Intifada; and impatience with what appears to be a lengthy peace process—these developments have frustrated many Palestinians and led them either to shun politics or to turn to impulsive radicalism.

Most Palestinians don't expect to see the establishment of their own independent state in the near future. At best, some form of autonomy is anticipated. Prior to the Israeli-PLO agreement in September 1993, journalists, UN and diplomatic personnel, and other observers reported a growing loss of faith in their own leaders among Palestinians. There was increasing disenchantment with Arafat and other top PLO leaders, and a widespread belief that they have capitalized on Palestinian suffering to achieve their own ends. After more than four years, the enthusiasm originally aroused by the Intifada had begun to peter out. There was a growing perception that the Intifada too had failed. Palestinians' sweeping support for Saddam Hussein was less an indication of belief in pan-Arabism than an indication of frustration and a turning toward radicalism. Many favored the Iraqi president because he seemed to put other Arab leaders on the spot.

Increasing support for Islamic fundamentalist factions among the Palestinians was still another indication of frustration with the impasse. Within the West Bank and Gaza, this frustration was evident in the increasing strength of Hamas and in numerous instances of cooperation between the fundamentalists and militant factions within the PLO that reject any form of political compromise.

Even after the accord, most Palestinians remained skeptical. A poll taken by the Center for Palestine Research and Studies in East Jerusalem just after announcement of the agreement indicated that although nearly two-thirds of Palestinians backed the accord only 45 percent believed that it would lead to a Palestinian state and attainment of Palestinian rights (*Christian Science Monitor*, September 14, 1993).

Israeli Occupation and the Gulf War

There is virtual unanimity among Palestinians and observers with whom I talked that Israel's occupation of the West Bank and Gaza must end. The occupation is regarded not only as intrusion into the lives of those under Israeli military authority, but as a burden on the larger Palestinian community. The occupation causes hardship for those directly exposed to its restrictions, its enforcement measures, and the discomforts of daily life under military rule, as well as for relatives abroad who suffer vicariously when they learn that their kin face frequent curfews, searches and seizures, a lack of civil law, punishment without trial, and the like.

As reports from the Occupied Territories circulated through Palestinian communities abroad, hostility toward Israel intensified and Palestinian attitudes about resolution of the conflict hardened. Such reports tend to exacerbate militant attitudes toward Israel, the UN, the United States, and even Arab governments, which appear to be unable to ameliorate the plight of those under Israeli rule. Occupation is seen as a major obstacle to development of the Palestinian potential. As long as the occupation continues, many believe it will be impossible for Palestinians to realize their own aspirations—to institute plans for economic and social development, to devise their own educational system and self-governing institutions, and to realize their full cultural potential. Only in a territory not subject to outside domination can the plans devised by Palestinian economists, educators, and political scientists be implemented.

Within the Occupied Territories, the Intifada has lost momentum. However, Palestinians abroad still perceive the uprising as a milestone on the road toward achieving national goals, and they regard it as a major achievement that has galvanized the community as no other event since the 1936–39 Arab revolt; it is perceived as a serious blow to Israel's economy, its self-confidence, and its continued string of political and military victories.

For similar reasons, there remains a large residue of sympathy toward Saddam Hussein. He is highly regarded by many, even more so than former Egyptian president Nasser or any Palestinian figure, because he dared to challenge the world powers, especially the United States, Israel's chief ally and major source of sustenance. Palestinians' support for Saddam is reinforced by the harsh treatment suffered by Palestinians in Kuwait and surrounding countries during and after the Gulf War. While some Palestinians did assist the invading Iraqis during 1990, informed Palestinian observers believe that they were a small minority. These observers say that most Palestinians in Kuwait did not give aid or comfort to the invaders, and many actively participated in the Kuwaiti resistance. The precipitous expulsion of Palestinians from Kuwait turned many Palestinians against the sheikhdom's rulers, who are considered corrupt and degenerate. Saddam Hussein, the enemy of the Kuwaiti rulers, is now seen in a favorable light.

The Peace Process

Having been through several peace negotiations since 1948 that produced few if any positive results for them, Palestinians are prepared to be disappointed again. Beginning with the Lausanne conferences in 1949, through the Eric Johnston and Joseph Johnson plans in the 1950s and 1960s, from Glassboro to Camp David, the Palestinians complain, they have gained nothing. But still, most supported the Madrid peace negotiations. The Jerusalem weekly *Al-Bayader al-Siyasi* polled 1,200 Palestinians in late 1991 on the question "Do you support the current peace negotiations?" Over 60 percent responded yes, 35.5 percent no, .05 percent no answer, and 4.1 percent no opinion. Seventy-six percent of the women supported the negotiations, as did 79 percent of the farmers and 68 percent of the villagers. Seventy-five percent of the older people, but only 55 percent of youths, supported the negotiations. Fifty-six percent of the clergy opposed the peace negotiations.

A number of Palestinians now have second thoughts about rejecting the autonomy proposals offered at Camp David in 1978 (the proposals called for a limited form of self-government for the West Bank and Gaza). Some acknowledge that those proposals represent a lost opportunity: Had they been acted on, the community would now be much closer to achieving its aspirations. Israel's present negotiating stance is similar to the Camp David plan. Those who acknowledge that Camp David represents a lost opportunity maintain that the plan was rejected because of the manner in which it was presented and because public opinion was not then prepared for such a plan. Egyptian president Anwar Sadat was so peremptory in extending the offer that to Palestinian leaders it seemed more like an insult than an opportunity.

Changes in the international environment and greater responsiveness to Palestinian sensitivities have made efforts to renew the peace process more acceptable. The end of the Cold War and the overall easing of tensions among the major powers enabled the Palestinians to evaluate the peace process more realistically. Rather than dividing the region between pro–United States and pro-Soviet clients, the new peace negotiations demonstrate cooperation in a region that was until recently one of the principal battlefields in the Cold War. Palestinians are acutely aware of the new international climate, and they realize that Moscow can no longer be used to counterbalance the United States–Israel entente. Some hopes were raised in August

1991 when it seemed that Soviet hard-liners were about to reassert their authority, renewing the decades-long competition in the Middle East. But the enthusiasm aroused by the failed coup quickly dissipated, and more realistic perceptions returned.

Quite obviously, the Gulf War was an important catalyst in reviving the peace process, even though the United States adamantly denied any link between its policy toward Iraq and the Arab-Israeli conflict. Iraq's defeat and the divisiveness caused by the war demonstrated that the Arab system was not working; solidarity in resistance to negotiations with Israel no longer existed. The major Arab states were far from unanimous in their attitudes toward negotiations with Israel; Palestinians, realizing that they stood alone, would now have to devise their own policies. As a result, Palestinian leaders became more amenable to American proposals and to Washington's tactics for reviving the peace process. Several Palestinian spokespersons expressed respect, even admiration, for the way the U.S. government prepared the scene. In 1978, Palestinians were confronted with Sadat's near-ultimatum demanding their participation; this time there was a gradual buildup to the 1991 Madrid talks, during which the various Arab parties were conditioned to accept the idea of direct negotiations.

Some Palestinians maintain that the process started during the Reagan administration with visits to the Middle East by Secretary of State George Shultz and Assistant Secretary Richard Murphy, who began to construct a new framework for peace. In subsequent visits to the region, Secretary of State James Baker built on the foundations laid by his predecessors. American officials now appeared to be more patient, engaging the parties in more discussion; they seemed more conscious of Arab and Palestinian sensitivities. According to some Palestinian leaders, the Arabs obtained well-constructed assurances about the conditions of participation and the overall framework of negotiations. This lengthy preparation and greater responsiveness to regional sensibilities, against the background of global and regional political and military conditions, led to success in the opening phases of the new peace effort.

Even many individuals and factions often characterized as "rejectionist" have not opposed the new peace initiative. Still, they have been highly critical of the conditions and terms of Palestinian participation. In March 1992, some 170 prominent members of the PNC signed an internal memorandum addressed to PLO chairman Arafat expressing concern about the limitations imposed on Palestinian participation.[20] Among their major objections were failure to include in the official delegation representatives of Palestinians outside the Occupied Territories, especially those from refugee camps (in the original Madrid delegation of over 50 individuals, none came from a refugee camp); failure to demand cessation of Jewish settlement in the territories, at least during the negotiating process; and failure to insist more forcefully on implementing the provision in UN Resolution 194 (III) calling for Palestinians to be allowed to return to homes within Israel.

Only a minority of Palestinians categorically oppose the peace process under any conditions. They can be divided into militant fundamentalists such as those affiliated with Hamas, and others whose conditions for participation are even farther beyond the bounds of political realism, such as dissident factions that are not a part of the PLO like Ahmed Jabril. It should be emphasized that not all Muslim religious leaders oppose peace negotiations and not all fundamentalists follow the rejectionist line of Hamas. Sheikh Abdul Hamid al Sayeh, speaker of the PNC, is a traditional Islamic cleric whose perceptions of current Middle East political realities are clouded by anachronistic slogans and images, but he too accepted the 1988 decision of the PNC to seek a two-state solution and pursue the peace process. The great danger is that tens of thousands of Palestinians are wavering on the fine line between Hamas and those clerics who have accepted the majority positions of the PNC calling for peaceful compromise.

Questions about the political and economic future of the Palestinians are intimately linked with the dispute over Jewish settlement in the territories. There is as much unanimity among Palestinians about this issue as there is on the need to end the occupation. Realists understand that the occupation will end not immediately but gradually, as part of a peace process. However, across the spectrum, from right to left, moderate to militant, secularist to fundamentalist, there is great anxiety about continued Jewish settlement. All Palestinian groups demand that it stop immediately. The realization that in 1991–92 the number of Jewish settlers increased by 60 percent and the pervasive physical evidence of proliferating housing developments throughout the West Bank frightened Palestinians. Further settlement, they argue, will preclude the possibility of establishing any form of Palestinian entity.

Attempts by the mainstream PLO leadership, principally Fatah, to encourage popular participation in decision making on issues of national importance have not always been successful. Efforts have been made within the Occupied Territories to elicit the views and participation of refugee camp inhabitants and villagers. Public meetings have been organized at various sites where open discussions have been held with delegates to the peace conference. These discussions have not always been conducted according to *Robert's Rules of Order*; on occasion, violent altercations have occurred between factions supporting negotiations and those opposed. The most frequent demand is to establish more firm conditions for Palestinian participation. In Jordanian refugee camps, similar public meetings have been arranged by *mukhtars* (quasi-official local representatives to the government), camp leaders, or informal chieftans who have arisen from the new generation of politically active youth. It remains to be seen whether these experiments with civil, nonofficial popular discussion of vital issues will develop into democratic fora for the open expression of diverse opinions.

Palestinians in the
West Bank and Gaza

By the early 1990s there were approximately 1,700,000 Palestinian Arabs in the Israeli-occupied West Bank (excluding East Jerusalem) and Gaza, over 1 million in the West Bank and over 600,000 in the Gaza Strip. About 470,000 Palestinians in the West Bank were classified by UNRWA as refugees, over 120,000 of whom were living in camps; the refugee population of the Gaza region was over 580,000, with more than 320,000 in camps. In each region there were two categories of Palestinians: the indigenous Arab population, whose families had lived in the West Bank and Gaza since mandatory times or before, and refugees who came from those parts of Palestine that became Israel during the 1947–48 exodus.

The 1 million Palestine refugees in the West Bank and Gaza Strip are still within the borders of Palestine, not in the diaspora. However, their conditions are often as difficult as, and at times worse than, conditions in the diaspora. Their prospects depend on the future political status of the Occupied Territories.

From the end of the mandate in 1948, when Palestine was divided into areas occupied by Egypt, Jordan, and Israel, until Israel occupied all of mandatory Palestine in 1967, Gaza was occupied by Egypt under the terms of the 1949 Israel-Egypt armistice agreement; the West Bank was under Jordanian control under the terms of the 1949 Israel-Jordan armistice agreement.

Gaza was under Egyptian military rule, although the Cairo authorities permitted local Palestinian organizations to exist, fostered a certain degree of local self-government, and co-opted Palestinians into paramilitary units. A small number of Palestinians, both refugees and others, were allowed into Egypt for higher education and employment. Some refugees in the Gaza region were employed by local land and factory owners, but by far the largest number of refugees were unemployed and depended for survival on assistance received from UNRWA. The refugees' unemployment and impoverished living conditions were a major cause of tensions between the refugees and the Egyptians and native Gazians. Refugee infiltration across the border into Israel, where many had owned farms, homes, and other property before the 1948 war, was one of the principal causes of border tensions between Israel and Egypt and was a factor leading to the 1956 and 1967 wars between Israel and Egypt. Because Gaza was never annexed by Egypt, Palestinians living there were not Egyptian citizens but stateless persons. (With the end of the mandate, Palestinian citizenship ceased to exist and the passports issued by the British mandatory authorities were no longer recognized for travel abroad.) Little was done to encourage the economic development of Gaza, and it became one of the most overcrowded and poverty-stricken areas of Palestine refugee concentration.

The situation of Palestinians, both refugees and others, living in the West Bank differed. King Abdullah annexed the West Bank in 1950 and its Palestinian population became Jordanian citizens. They were represented in Jordan's parliament and many held high government offices (see "Jordan," below).

In June 1967 Israel occupied Gaza and the West Bank, placing both regions under military government. Jordanian East Jerusalem was separated from the West Bank and Israeli law was imposed a few days after the conquest in June 1967. Thus Arabs in East (formerly Jordanian) Jerusalem were given the option of becoming Israeli citizens, an option that not more than a few score accepted. Although Israel considers East Jerusalem and additional West Bank areas adjoining it part of the state of Israel, the Arab inhabitants of these areas have not accepted integration into the Jewish state.

Until implementation of the 1993 agreement between Israel and the PLO, Gaza and the West Bank will continue to be ruled under martial law, each region under a different Israeli military governor. Both regions are subject to the restrictions imposed by the military authorities noted above under "Israeli Occupation and the Gulf War." Living conditions in the Occupied Territories in terms of employment, wages, material acquisitions such as automobiles and televisions, and upper- and middle-class housing construction have improved under occupation, largely as a result of Palestinian employment in Israel; however, the economies of both the West Bank and Gaza have become mere adjuncts to Israel's economy. Economic difficulties and problems created by Israeli occupation are examined below in "Return to a Palestinian State," page 75.

The agreement between Israel and the PLO signed in September 1993 resembled the 1978 Camp David agreement between Israel and Egypt providing for Palestinian autonomy in Gaza and the West Bank. However, the Camp David autonomy plan was never implemented. The 1993 agreement provided for a five-year transitional period during which Israel would redeploy its forces outside Arab-populated areas in Gaza and the West Bank, although Israel would continue to be responsible for security of Jewish settlers and settlements in the Occupied Territories. During the transitional period, many governmental and administrative functions that had been controlled by the Israeli military government would be transferred to Palestinian authorities. The Palestinians would elect a council to manage a Palestinian Interim Self-Government Authority (PISGA), which would be responsible for education and culture, health, social welfare, taxation, and tourism in the Arab sector. A Palestinian police force would be organized to assume responsibility for Palestinian security, although Israeli forces would continue to be responsible for Jewish areas of settlement as well as external security. Initially Israeli withdrawals or redeployment of troops would occur only in Gaza and the Jericho region but the intent would be to eventually apply the agreement to all the West Bank.

The five-year transitional period would begin with Israeli withdrawal from Gaza and the Jericho area. Within two years Israel and the Palestinians were to begin negotiations to determine the final status of Gaza and the West Bank, with the goal of concluding negotiations at the end of the five-year period. The question of Jerusalem's future status was deferred until final status negotiations. The interim agreement also included protocols calling for Israeli-Palestinian cooperation in economic and development programs.

While opinion polls indicated wide support for the new agreement in both Israel and among the Palestinians, opposition was strong. Islamic fundamentalists in Hamas and militant nationalists in the Popular Front for the Liberation of Palestine and in the Democratic Front seemed determined to prevent implementation. In addition to problems of internal security raised by opposition factions, there were difficulties to be met in organizing a self-governing administration and in financing autonomy (see page 83).

Palestinians in the Diaspora

Of the 2.7 million refugees registered with UNRWA in 1992, over 1.6 million were located in the Palestinian diaspora, in the host countries of Jordan, Lebanon, and Syria. In addition to those registered as refugees with UNRWA, more than half a million Palestinians were located in other Arab countries where, although not classified as refugees, they were unable to obtain local citizenship. Many of them held Jordanian passports but had lived outside Jordan for most of their lives. While many prospered economically, their situation as noncitizens in places such as Kuwait and Saudi Arabia was precarious. The Gulf War in 1990–91 precipitated a new crisis in the situation when hundreds of thousands were forced to leave several of the Gulf states. The largest exodus was from Kuwait.

Jordan

Jordan has received the largest number of Palestinian refugees. Within the past 45 years, there have been three major waves. In the first wave, during 1947–48, more than 100,000 Palestinians fled to what was then Transjordan and over 350,000 went to the West Bank, which was occupied by Transjordanian forces. During and immediately after the 1967 war, 120,000 Palestinians who had become refugees in 1947–48 left the West Bank and East Jerusalem for East

Jordan. Nearly 200,000 more fled for the first time from the West Bank to East Jordan in 1967. They were not technically counted as refugees but as displaced persons, because Jordan still claimed sovereignty over the West Bank; thus they fled from one part of the country to another. During 1990–91, more than 300,000 Palestinians, most of them with Jordanian passports, returned to Jordan from Kuwait, Iraq, Saudi Arabia, and other Gulf states. Although they were Jordanian citizens and not refugees in a technical sense, the last group relocated in such haste that for all practical purposes their situation on arrival in Jordan was that of refugees.

After the union of the East and West Bank as the new Hashemite Kingdom of Jordan in 1950, Palestinians became approximately half of the country's population. From 1950 until 1988, there was no official distinction in citizenship status between Jordanian citizens of Palestinian origin and others; thus, it was difficult to obtain an accurate count of the number of Jordanians who were Palestinians. Current unofficial estimates by Jordanian, UNRWA, and other observers range from 45 to 60 percent of the total population.

After the West Bank was annexed in 1950, the Hashemite rulers attempted to "Jordanize" their new subjects and made strenuous efforts to obliterate a distinctive Palestinian consciousness within the kingdom. Palestinians ascended to the highest positions in government, becoming generals in the army, cabinet officers, and even prime ministers. Some officials claim that a majority of the country's civil servants are of Palestinian origin. Palestinian businessmen prospered in Jordan, investing in agriculture, industry, trade, and finance. The Arab Bank, the country's largest financial institution, was owned and managed by Palestinians.

The addition of the West Bank, East Jerusalem, and the Palestinian population on both sides of the river changed Jordan from a desert principality into a full-fledged kingdom. The initial gap in education, income, and social status between Palestinians, who were mostly of rural or urban origin, and the Transjordanians, who were mostly of Bedouin origin, has been closed. However, some distinctions still remain, and many Palestinians believe that indigenous East Bankers receive preference in economic, political, and social matters.

During the 17 years that the West Bank and East Jerusalem were part of the Hashemite Kingdom of Jordan, priority in economic development was given to the East Bank and to Jordan's capital, Amman. East Bank investors received economic benefits unavailable to those in the West Bank. Government activity, industrial and other development projects, and cultural and higher educational institutions were in the East Bank, and few of the country's resources were allocated to the West Bank. For example, although Jerusalem is considered the third most holy city in Islam, live broadcasts of Friday prayers came from the central mosque in Amman rather than from al-Aqsa Mosque in Jerusalem. The royal family had no official residence in Jerusalem, and it was not until shortly before the 1967 war that construction was begun there on a residence for the king.

West Bank Palestinians were divided politically between supporters of the Hashemites and Palestinian nationalists. Many notables from old, established, well-to-do families who had opposed the mufti of Jerusalem, Haj Amin al-Husseini, during the mandate were among the pro-Hashemites. They included such well-known names as the Nashashibis, the Khalidis, and the Dajanis from Jerusalem as well as a number of regional figures such as the al-Masris of Nablus and the al-Jabris of Hebron. Many of them obtained high posts in the Jordanian government.

The Palestinian opposition to the Hashemites, led by the Husseinis and other followers of the former mufti, favored the establishment of a Palestinian state; their militant nationalism often led to clashes with Jordanian security forces. The opposition also included young political activists who formed Jordanian branches of the Ba'ath, the Muslim Brotherhood, and the Communist and Socialist parties. Many of them were imprisoned between 1947 and 1967. There was no love lost between a large part of the Palestinian community and the royal family.

Possibilities of improved economic conditions attracted many West Bank Palestinians to Amman and other East Bank towns during the mandate. A small number of Palestinians had joined the Jordanian administration before 1947, among them several members of the Rifai family, who became some of the closest advisors to the Hashemites.

Between 1947 and 1967, an estimated half-million people left the West Bank; most settled in Amman. Several hundred thousand continued their eastward trek to the Gulf in search of economic security.

Palestinian settlement in Amman made the capital into Jordan's primary city, containing nearly a quarter of the country's population. "The size and trend of migration to Amman was linked, to a great extent, to the movement of refugees, which represented over one-half of migration to the city."[21] In a 1977 survey, refugees represented 40 percent of the migrants. By 1991, refugees were about half the population in each of Jordan's three largest cities, Amman, Zarqa, and Irbid.

Until 1967, Jordanian policy tended to repress overt manifestations of Palestinian nationalism; however, Israel's conquest of East Jerusalem and the West Bank led to changing relationships between Palestinians and the Jordanian authorities. By 1969, King Hussein publicly endorsed autonomy for the Palestinians within the Hashemite Kingdom of Jordan. In 1972, he offered self-government in a proposal calling for a confederation with two legislatures, one for the Palestinians in the West Bank and another for those in the East Bank, both subordinate to a supreme parliament for the kingdom as a whole. Each regional legislature would be responsible for local matters; defense and foreign affairs would remain the prerogative of the central authority. Both the Israeli government (then occupying the West Bank) and the PLO rejected the proposal. Since then, Israel's Labor Party has periodically called for a solution with some elements of Palestinian self-rule within a Jordanian context. The PLO, too, has reversed its position.

After 1967, relations between the Jordanian government and the Palestinians were in a constant state of flux. At times King Hussein negotiated and signed agreements with the PLO; at other times, the organization and its leaders were banned from the country. During the most severe crisis, the Palestinian uprising in 1970–71, all commando forces were driven from the country and the offices of most Palestinian political factions were closed.

After the outbreak of the Intifada in December 1987, it became evident that by far the largest number of Palestinians favored establishment of an independent state and that any political association with Jordan would be dependent on free choice by the Palestinians themselves. King Hussein reacted to the Intifada by withdrawing Jordanian responsibility for the West Bank in 1988. The Jordanian Ministry for the Occupied Territories was closed and its duties turned over to a less prestigious office in the foreign ministry. Salaries paid by Jordan to West Bank officials and government employees, except for those in Muslim institutions, were slashed. The lower house of Jordan's parliament, half of whose members were Palestinians, was dissolved. Finally, the king officially gave up all claims to the West Bank and turned over responsibility to the PLO, symbolizing his recognition of an independent Palestinian state.

Since the Intifada, amicable relations have been reestablished and several Palestinian national organizations have reopened offices in Amman. Jordan and the Palestinians formed a single delegation at the Madrid peace conference, giving full support to Palestinian demands for the election of a self-governing body in the West Bank and Gaza and for the complete withdrawal of Israel from the Occupied Territories.

At present, Palestinians in the East Bank can be divided into three principal groups. Those in the camps, by and large, do not feel Jordanian in any sense but regard themselves as Palestinians living in exile. They have little affection for King Hussein or respect for his government. A second group, represented by mainstream Palestinian nationalists, accepts the status quo but demands that more vigorous efforts be made to establish a Palestinian state. This group recognizes exile as a condition to be put up with for the moment but looks forward to eventual "return" to a Palestine state. A third group has been assimilated into the mainstream of society as Jordanians of Palestinian origin. They too support establishment of a Palestinian state, but their primary loyalty is to Jordan.

Confederation

In recent months, discussion about confederation between a prospective Palestinian entity and Jordan has gained momentum. Some

Palestinians feel they can live with the idea once their right of self-determination is obtained; others see confederation as the immediate answer to a political settlement. The PLO mainstream has accepted the possibility of confederation and included it in the political communiqué issued by the PNC at its meeting in Algiers in November 1988. The communiqué states that the PNC acknowledges "the distinctive relationship between the Jordanian and Palestinian peoples, and affirms that the future relationship between the two states of Palestine and Jordan should be on a confederal basis as a result [of] the free and voluntary choice of the two fraternal peoples."[22]

Among proponents of immediate confederation are many who, having become part of Jordan's ruling establishment, now identify themselves as Jordanians of Palestinian origin. Some of them believe it possible to skip the intermediate step of a separate Palestinian entity. Some feel that there will never be a Palestinian state; however, confederation is not too unrealistic an objective.

The issue was raised in March 1992 when Arafat's political advisor, Nabil Shaath, observed that the PLO had committed itself to the creation of a confederation in its November 1988 political communiqué (p. 55). Details were discussed with Jordan, but the plan would be implemented only on the basis of parity between two equal partners, and only after a final peace settlement. Also in March 1992, the 17-member Fatah Central Committee held extensive discussions on confederation, agreeing that a phased approach should be attempted. Faruq Qaddumi, head of the PLO Political Department, proposed that confederation be voted on in a referendum among both Jordanians and Palestinians after establishment of a Palestinian state.[23]

Confederation would substantially increase the political strength of Palestinians, already a major force in Jordan. For this reason, some East Bank Jordanians are not enthusiastic about confederation. The threat of Palestinian political predominance was a factor in Prime Minister Rifai's advice to King Hussein that he "disengage" from the West Bank in 1988.

Confederation would contribute to a psychological easing of the refugee situation by reinforcing the Jordanian-Palestinian identity of the approximately 2 million refugees in Jordan and the Occupied Territories; after confederation, they would be located in a new political entity with which they could all identify.

The plan would give strategic depth to a Palestinian entity; a state or autonomous unit formed from the West Bank and Gaza alone, a total area of some 2,500 square miles, would be a strategic nightmare, incapable of military defense against its much more powerful neighbors. The concept of a Palestinian-Jordanian confederation that later might be expanded to include Israel and/or surrounding Arab countries is not discounted by Palestinians with vision. Such a three-state confederation was proposed several years ago by Shimon Peres. However, even Palestinians willing to contemplate this far-reaching concept insist that public discussion must await a final comprehensive peace settlement.

Since the Gulf War, the situation of Palestinians in Jordan has greatly worsened. The addition of another 300,000 persons to the country's refugee population has undermined prospects for improving the economic position of the whole country and placed in jeopardy plans for development that were already on the drawing board. (See "Resettlement" below.)

Paradoxically, despite 20 percent unemployment, there are still more than 100,000 foreign workers (mostly Egyptians) in Jordan in low-paid, unskilled jobs such as agriculture, construction, and services. These imported workers arrived during the period of economic expansion in the 1970s and early 1980s when more than 300,000 Jordanian-Palestinians found highly paid work abroad, mostly in the Gulf. Many left with their families; thus the total number of expatriates was between 800,000 and 1 million. Palestinians who returned as a result of the Gulf War and most of the Palestinian refugees are still reluctant to replace the unskilled Egyptians despite the uncertainty of employment in the camps.

Kuwait

Large numbers of Palestinians began to arrive in Kuwait soon after the 1948 war when the sheikhdom, still a British protectorate, started to develop its economy. The new arrivals included both skilled workers with contracts and unskilled workers who entered the country illegally. Between 1949 and 1967, Kuwait's population more than doubled, from 100,000 to more than 200,000, as a result of imported labor. By the first census in 1957, non-Kuwaitis had become nearly 45 percent of the population. Iranians and Iraqis were the largest immigrant groups, with Palestinians and Jordanians following, although the latter were seen as potentially providing the greatest number of immigrants.

When oil production began to rise in the 1950s, providing huge capital resources, the Kuwaiti government initiated a development program as the basis for rapid expansion of the total economy. Palestinians became a major source of labor at all levels; they were especially useful in commerce because of their knowledge of English.

To facilitate the entry of foreign workers, Kuwait signed a number of agreements with other Arab states annulling visa requirements. An agreement with Jordan canceled the requirement for visas for those who were Jordanian citizens in 1958–59. This led to an influx of Palestinians from both the East and West Banks, where economic conditions had become difficult. After establishing themselves in Kuwait, many Palestinians brought in not only their immediate families but other relatives and friends, thus starting a large Palestinian community that remained in the country for more than 30 years.

Palestinians who ascended to influential posts facilitated the entry of many others from towns, villages, and refugee camps in their native Palestine or Jordan. Many businesses and government departments employed Palestinians brought to Kuwait by friends or relatives who had acquired authority. The ministries of public works and electricity became well known for their large Palestinian staffs, the latter nicknamed *musta'mar yafawi*, or Jaffa colony.[24]

Long-time residence in Kuwait did not ensure Palestinians citizenship or the right to permanent residence. Migration and citizenship laws differentiated between native Kuwaitis and "newcomers." While ensuring the relatively free immigration of labor in times of need (an objective supported by the Kuwaiti merchant elite), the

government insisted on control over the entry, movement, and employment of aliens through a system of work and residence permits.

Nationality law placed severe restrictions on the acquisition of
citizenship. The original law permitted only 50 new naturalizations
a year. Later, the 1960 law required Arabs, with few exceptions, to
have 10 years' residence before becoming eligible for citizenship.
Even acquisition of citizenship did not provide full equality. A sharp
distinction was made between naturalized and "original" Kuwaitis:
Both categories were eligible for civil service employment, property
ownership, education, and a wide range of other benefits, but naturalized citizens could not vote until 20 years after becoming citizens,
nor were they eligible for appointment to a representative body or
ministerial position.[25]

Similar legislation ensured that economic control and most business profits would remain in Kuwaiti hands. Although noncitizens
could join Kuwaiti labor unions after five consecutive years of work
in Kuwait, they could not vote in union elections. Non-Kuwaitis
could join professional organizations, but they could not vote or be
elected to office in those organizations. In industry, at least 51 percent
of any company had to be controlled by Kuwaitis; non-Kuwaitis were
banned from establishing banking and financial institutions.

By law, non-Kuwaitis had to leave the country upon termination
of their employment. Even if a company wished to continue or renew
a worker's employment, it was limited in the number of resident
workers it could sponsor. When the oil boom of the early and mid-
1970s slowed down, Kuwait's economy began to cool off. Many companies began to lay off employees and "temporary" workers as the
need for imported labor declined. When workers from other countries were required to return to their homelands, Palestinians were
unable to go home. Even those with Jordanian passports often faced
difficulties because few had any real base or home in Jordan. A
Jordanian passport was more a document of convenience than an
indication of real identity.

When a new influx of Palestinians arrived after the June 1967 war,
the Kuwaiti government again tightened its immigration policy.
Authorities feared the spread of political radicalism and repercussions

from events occurring elsewhere in the Arab world, such as the growing tensions between Palestinians and King Hussein in Jordan. Attempts were made to keep out "dissidents" and to crack down on "security risks" within Kuwait. The slowdown of immigration resulted in a drop in the population growth rate from over 10 percent before 1965 to 2 percent by the early 1970s.[26]

Another government objective was to strengthen the ratio of Kuwaiti citizens to non-Kuwaitis. This was accomplished by increasing the number of naturalized citizens. Between 1961 and 1970 the number of naturalized citizens constituted over a quarter of the total Kuwaiti population. This helped to preserve the 1965 ratio of 48 percent Kuwaitis to 52 percent non-Kuwaitis. Work and residence permits could be acquired only at the request of a Kuwaiti through the Ministry of the Interior or the Ministry of Social Affairs. Kuwaiti employers were thus made responsible for their non-Kuwaiti employees in all legal and financial matters.[27]

The oil boom of the early 1970s led to renewed demand for foreign workers. Now, however, employers gave preference to Asians, whose wage rates were considerably lower than those in the Arab labor markets. As the number of Asian workers increased, there was a decline in the percentage of Palestinian-Jordanian arrivals.

Sociopolitical considerations became a dominant feature of immigration policy. By the 1980s, Kuwaiti authorities were concerned about the increasing radicalism, including bombings within the country and attacks on Kuwaiti property and installations abroad. The 1979 revolution in Iran and the growing strength of religious conservatives in the Kuwaiti National Assembly also aroused apprehension in the ruling establishment.

It was increasingly evident that "temporary" migrants were becoming long-term, if not permanent, residents. Government figures revealed that nearly a third of non-Kuwaitis had been in the country for ten or more years; nearly 16 percent had been resident for fifteen or more years. The latest census showed that nearly 30 percent (more than 300,000) of the non-Kuwaitis had been born in the country. Furthermore, the percentage of Kuwaitis had declined to 40 percent of the total population.[28]

An estimated 95 percent of Jordanians in Kuwait were Palestinian. Between 1957 and 1970, the percentage of Palestinian-Jordanians rose from 16 percent of the immigrant population and 7.3 percent of the total population to 37.7 percent and 20 percent, respectively. Estimates based on Jordanian figures indicated that the number of Palestinians from Jordan was five times as high in Kuwait as in any other Arab country.[29]

Laurie Brand divides the Palestinian community residing in Kuwait into former farmers and unskilled and semiskilled low-income workers; a small group of skilled workers of modest income, including government employees; and the middle and upper middle class, including those in the private sector and small businesses and professionals such as journalists, engineers, physicians, lawyers, and teachers. Although there were a small number of very wealthy Palestinians in Kuwait, the great majority lived modestly. In many Palestinian families, both husband and wife worked; often bread-winners held two or more jobs because of Kuwait's high cost of living and inflation. Palestinian residential areas, some characteristically named "West Bank" or "Gaza," were far from luxurious.

In Kuwait, as in other diaspora centers, Palestinian society remained cohesive and Palestinian identity was deeply rooted. When the Kuwaiti government imposed a limit on the number of non-Kuwaitis who could enroll in schools, Palestinians opened their own private schools. Because the number of Palestinians increased at such a rapid rate in the late 1960s, the PLO placed continuing pressure on the government to increase the Palestinian quota. In 1967, the PLO reached an agreement with the government permitting the organization to operate its own schools with assistance from the Kuwaiti authorities. Although these schools faced financial problems, they succeeded in instilling a Palestinian national consciousness in their students. The PLO schools were closed after the 1976–77 academic year, and the children returned to government schools; however, the authorities limited entry to children of expatriates who had been in the country as of January 1, 1963. Despite funds raised by private organizations to provide tuition, the problem of educating Palestinian children in Kuwait remained.

Until the Gulf War, relations between the Palestinian community and the Kuwaiti government were relatively good. Palestinians even volunteered to serve in the Kuwaiti armed forces during threatening times. Palestinians had influence in the bureaucracy, but as the number of Kuwaitis in government increased, Palestinian influence declined. Political life was relatively free and government intervention in the media and in academic life was less pervasive than in most of the Arab world. Thus, Palestinian journalists and writers in Kuwait had more opportunity for free expression than those in many other Middle East countries.[30]

Relations between the Kuwaiti government and Palestinian nationalist groups were friendly. Fatah was permitted to organize and had its headquarters in Kuwait until it moved to Damascus in 1966. From the late 1960s, the Kuwaiti government collected a 5-percent "liberation tax" on the salaries of Palestinian employees. The tax was turned over to the Palestine National Fund to finance the various activities of the PNC and PLO. During the internecine fighting among Palestinian factions after 1983, the overwhelming majority of the community remained loyal to PLO leader Arafat.

A variety of Palestinian social and cultural organizations were active in Kuwait. An exception was made to the rule banning non-Kuwaiti labor unions, and the General Union of Palestine Workers was permitted to function as an affiliate of the PLO. Palestinians were also permitted to organize a council to coordinate the activities of their various unions, political groups, and women's, teachers', and students' organizations. Activities included a periodic Conference of Palestinian Popular Organizations that debated political and social issues and sponsored cultural activities to strengthen national solidarity. According to Laurie Brand,

> It was the Palestinians more than any other single expatriate group who helped shape the country's social, economic, and political development. The length of their residence, the size of the community, their dedication to work in both the public and private sectors, and their consequent entrenchment in the bureaucracy, economy, professions, and the media enabled the Palestinians in Kuwait to develop into one of the most cohesive and active communities in the diaspora.[31]

Precisely because it had been so successful, Kuwait's Palestinian community felt the effects of the Gulf War all the more keenly.

Relationships between the Kuwaiti authorities and the Palestinian community were influenced by events in the larger Middle East context, at times creating tensions between the government and the Palestinian leadership. Palestinian reactions to the insurrection in Jordan during 1970–71 and in Lebanon during the late 1970s and 1980s raised concern among Kuwaiti authorities. Although Kuwait had consistently supported the Palestinians at the UN and in international fora and had provided financial assistance to the PLO and emergency funds during the Lebanese civil war, the large numbers of Palestinians and their positions of influence at critical locations in Kuwaiti society made them suspect in the way that powerful minorities often are.

The enthusiasm among many Palestinians for Saddam Hussein and his attack on Kuwait led to the assumption by Kuwait's rulers that "their Palestinians" had become a fifth column. Almost overnight, the decades-long relationships between resident Palestinians and Kuwaiti officials degenerated into head-on confrontation. Rumors quickly spread that Palestinians had stabbed Kuwait in the back, actually assisting the Iraqis in their assault on the native Kuwaiti population. No figures exist as to the reliability of these accusations; Kuwaitis who remained in the country believe that roughly 10 percent of the Palestinians collaborated with the occupiers, another 10 percent assisted the Kuwaiti underground resistance, and the rest merely followed orders of the Iraqi military or continued their pre-invasion activities as workers, students, and so forth. However, the Kuwaitis expected all residents to boycott work or to actively oppose the invasion, and so the perception of Palestinian collaboration prevailed. The result was that after the war, most Palestinians who remained in the country were treated as traitors.[32]

Estimates of the number of Palestinians in Kuwait before Iraq's invasion ranged from just over 300,000 to 400,000. At least half fled during and immediately after the invasion, mostly to Jordan. Some 25,000 returned to the Israeli-occupied West Bank, and another 7,000 returned to homes in Gaza.[33]

Since the war, Kuwait has adopted a policy of getting rid of Palestinians and other remaining "undesirables." There is certainly no intention of permitting those who left to return. In February 1992, Ibrahim al-Shatti, the *chef de cabinet* of Kuwait's Emir, Sheikh Jaber al-Ahmed al-Sabah, declared that Palestinians who left the country should be absorbed by Jordan because they held Jordanian passports. Jordanians and Palestinians from Kuwait were traitors who had betrayed Kuwait's generosity, he declared. "I must make particular mention of the Palestinians who lived in Kuwait" and because of the country's wealth and bounty "became filled with spite and hatred toward Kuwait." These Palestinians, charged al-Shatti, had also betrayed their own country: "In reality they ran away from Palestine for no reason, without a war. . . . The problem lies with the Palestinian people, who have no loyalty, unlike for example the Lebanese, Syrian, and Egyptian peoples." Lebanese, Syrians, and Egyptians who worked in Kuwait stayed for a few years and then returned to their homes; the Palestinians, al-Shatti charged, not only forgot their homeland but even refused to contribute to the Palestinian cause.[34]

The Kuwaiti program to rid the country of "undesirables" included terminating contracts of non-Kuwaiti public-sector employees, expelling from schools foreign children who had attended classes during the Iraqi occupation, even deporting non-Kuwaitis who committed serious traffic offenses.[35] By mid-1992, less than 40,000 of the prewar Palestinian population remained, and government officials stated that the number would be brought down to 10,000 or 15,000 as soon as possible. Kuwait's minister of planning, Ahmad al-Jassar, announced that his objective was to double the percentage of Kuwaiti citizens even if this necessitated a halt in the expansion of nonoil enterprises. In January 1992 Jassar put the country's total population at just over 1 million, compared with the prewar total of 2.2 million. Palestinians were excluded from receiving any of the 475,000 visas granted to non-Kuwaitis after the war ended in February 1991. In an effort to strengthen native Kuwaiti participation in the economy, government ministries were ordered to cut expatriate workforces to below 35 percent of the prewar level; the government workforces were reduced from 142,000 to 38,000.[36]

Lebanon

Until the expulsion of Palestinians from Kuwait during the Gulf War, Lebanon was the host country least hospitable to Palestine refugees. Unlike the Jordanian government, which had a calculated policy of integrating the refugees as citizens, the Lebanese government prevented Palestinians from being absorbed. From their arrival in 1947–48, Palestinians, constituting about 10 percent of the total population, were viewed by the Lebanese ruling establishment as a threat to internal political and social stability. Nevertheless, the 90 percent of the Palestinian population classified as refugees (about half of whom were in UNRWA camps) were often exploited as cheap labor during periods when Lebanon's economy was booming and when there were shortages of unskilled workers.

The great majority of Palestinians in Lebanon are stateless; their status is similar to that of Palestinians living in Gaza, who have no passports and who have been unable to acquire any recognized citizenship since the end of the mandate in 1948. Exceptions were made for about 3,000 mostly wealthy Christian Palestinians who received citizenship when Camille Chamoun was president between 1952 and 1958.[37] But the refugees "are regarded as being in Lebanon on sufferance. They are not granted residence visas and are not entitled to take advantage of the laws of citizenship. They have no political rights and no military obligations."[38] The principal reason for this policy has been a fear that Palestinians, more than 80 percent of whom are Muslims, would disturb the delicate balance between Lebanese Christians and Muslims, a balance that until recently was the basis of the country's political system.

Palestinians are subject to all laws pertaining to non-Lebanese in matters of employment, acquisition of property, taxation, and the like because the government considers them foreigners. They must obtain presidential consent to acquire immovable property. To be lawfully employed for a salary, or to be self-employed in commerce, industry, agriculture, or professions such as law and medicine, they must possess a *permis de travail* obtained from the Ministry of National Economy.

Because of the bureaucratic difficulties in obtaining labor permits, tens of thousands of Palestinians work for below minimum wage as black-market unskilled workers in construction, agriculture, and services. Most black-market workers are refugees living in the "misery belt," the slum areas surrounding Beirut and other Lebanese cities where many refugee camps are located. As in refugee camps elsewhere, there is a lower middle class or petty bourgeoisie living from trade and commerce in the camps or from work as clerks or merchants or in small businesses in the nearby towns.

Lebanon's supply-side economy and its free-market policies attracted hundreds of Palestinian investors and venture capitalists. Palestinians have been prominent in banking, as owners of airline companies and cinemas, and in auditing, marketing, and other technical services. Many played a pivotal role in developing Lebanon's economy between the 1950s and the 1970s. Because of their knowledge of English, many were hired by American companies with headquarters in Beirut prior to the civil war. One of the largest Palestinian enterprises was the Intra-Bank, which crashed during 1966 in mysterious circumstances. After the 1960s, the boom in Lebanon's Palestinian economy ended; many Palestinian businessmen believed that the collapse of the Intra-Bank proved the government's bias against them. The 15-year-long civil war also undermined confidence, and it physically destroyed most of Beirut's business, trade, and commerce.

The Lebanese government's treatment of the Palestinians inevitably created in them strong feelings of national solidarity and identification with opposition groups. These feelings were intensified when many members of commando movements expelled from Jordan in 1970–71 found refuge in Lebanon. By 1975, most Palestinians from all classes and sectors of society supported one or another of the organizations affiliated with the PLO.

After 1970, south Lebanon became the principal base of Palestinian commando operations against Israel, and refugee camps in south Lebanon were, for all practical purposes, run by commando groups free of control by Lebanese authorities. This situation caused increasing altercations between Palestinians and the Lebanese government, bringing the country close to civil war. Several other Arab countries became involved diplomatically, and in November 1969, Egyptian president Nasser mediated an agreement to suspend hostilities. The Cairo Agreement guaranteed Palestinians the right to "work, residence, and movement" in Lebanon and the right to "participate in the Palestinian revolution." The PLO was also authorized to engage in guerrilla attacks on Israel from specified regions in the south, but only in coordination with the Lebanese army.[39]

Rashid Khalidi observed that from 1968 until 1982, "Palestinians in Lebanon enjoyed a higher degree of autonomous control over their own affairs than any of their compatriots have since the beginning of the British mandate in Palestine. During this 14-year period, they developed social and cultural institutions, organs of self-government and security, and a powerful economic presence, mainly private, but also including a significant centrally directed sector." Except for the short period when they took over the camps in Jordan, this was the first time "significant numbers of Palestinians were almost entirely their own masters."[40]

Political differences and divisions within the Palestinian community erupted into violence in the refugee camps during the mid-1980s when various factions fought each other for control of the national movement in Lebanon. After Arafat and the PLO leadership were driven from Beirut by Israel in 1982, there was a major uprising in northern camps against Arafat's leadership, led by one of his former lieutenants. The anti-Arafat units were backed and supplied by Syria, reflecting the hostility between Syrian president Hafez al-Assad and Arafat and the mainstream PLO. The hostility was caused by policy differences and by Assad's attempts to control the Palestine national movement and subordinate it to Syrian policy objectives.

The gradual restoration of a Palestinian military presence in refugee camps and in south Lebanon after Israel's 1982 invasion led to a confrontation between PLO commando units and the Shi'ite Amal militia, backed by Syria. Vicious battles were waged between PLO units in the camps and Amal during the Battle of the Camps (1985–88). The siege imposed on the camps by Amal had a devastating impact on the Palestinian community; the conflict was also related to Syrian attempts to gain control of the Palestine national movement.

When UNRWA services declined because of a lack of adequate funding in the 1970s, the PLO provided social welfare assistance and an array of facilities including hospitals and clinics, orphanages, and preschool and day-care centers to the families of those killed in action. The PLO also took charge of security in Palestinian communities throughout the country, and in south Lebanon the organization extended its control over many areas surrounding the refugee camps. Palestinian commando attacks on northern Israel led to repeated retaliations by Israel, culminating in the massive invasion during the summer of 1982. A major motivation for the invasion was an attempt to finally destroy the PLO, which Israeli defense minister Ariel Sharon blamed for unrest in the West Bank and Gaza.

Since 1982, Lebanon has been in turmoil caused by internecine struggles among the various Lebanese militias, conflicts among Palestinian commando groups, repeated Israeli incursions, and Syrian military intervention. The Gulf War caused a further decline in living conditions among refugees in Lebanon because of the loss of remittances from and employment opportunities in most of the Gulf states. The end of the civil war led to the return of thousands of Lebanese from overseas, many now competing for jobs with unemployed Palestinians. Since the end of internal fighting and the extension of centralized authority, the new Lebanese government has tended to enforce more strictly laws and regulations that prevented Palestinians from working. Additional competition in the labor market has come from the thousands of young men discharged from the militias. According to an informed estimate by a UN official, most of those discharged from the Palestinian militias were refugees. A rough estimate is that in the near future, 37 percent of Palestinian men between the ages of 18 and 60 are likely to be unemployed; the total could be as high as 40,000.[41]

UNRWA greatly expanded its emergency assistance in Lebanon in the last few years because of this political instability. Israeli air raids extensively damaged facilities and caused many refugee casualties. Thousands of Palestinians fled from camps in the south to other locations within Lebanon. According to a UN source, tens of thousands have been displaced "over and over again. . . . At certain points, almost half . . . were displaced at least once."[42]

UNRWA's emergency programs provided additional food rations, medical aid to Palestinians wounded in the fighting, and help for refugees whose shelters were damaged or destroyed. UNRWA also provided emergency assistance to all other needy Palestinians as well as to impoverished Lebanese living in the vicinity of the Palestinians.

Following the restoration of a central government and the disarming of most militias, Lebanese authorities again had to confront the problem of Palestinians within the country. The Taif agreement (a "National Reconciliation Pact" signed at Taif, Saudi Arabia, in 1989 to end the Lebanese civil war and establish a new government) made no specific mention of the Palestinians or of the refugee problem. However, enforcement of the agreement meant disarming the Palestinians as well as the Lebanese militias. The Taif agreement also required that Lebanese government authority be reimposed on all parts of the country including Palestinian camps and other population centers. In south Lebanon, however, the government has been unable to impose its authority on the fundamentalist Party of God (Hezbollah), which continued its attacks on Israeli forces occupying a 15-mile-wide "Security Zone." The attacks resulted in massive Israeli retaliation and displacement of tens of thousands of people, many of them Palestine refugees.

The official position of the Lebanese government is that the Palestinians should have the "right of return" (see "Repatriation" below), although refugees now in the country may stay until they obtain their own country. No new refugees may enter Lebanon, nor may camps destroyed in recent military actions be rebuilt. There seems to be a willingness to permit only the economically self-sufficient to remain. The future of Palestinians in Lebanon depends on how many can be absorbed in a self-governing Palestinian entity. (See "Prospects for Solution" below.)

Syria

About 90 percent of the approximately 300,000 Palestinians in Syria are classified as refugees by UNRWA's definition. About 85,000 of them live in refugee camps, most adjoining or within Damascus, Hama, or

Deraa. The refugees are much less a burden to Syria than to Jordan or Lebanon. Since they number less than 3 percent of the population, they have not presented serious competition to native Syrians for scarce jobs. Furthermore, when the Palestinians first appeared in 1947–48, the country was underpopulated, and many economists saw the new arrivals as an asset for development in areas such as the Jezirah. In 1949, Prime Minister Husni Za'im proposed that Syria resettle 300,000 Palestine refugees as part of an overall resolution of the Arab-Israeli conflict. It was believed that he intended to settle them in sparsely inhabited regions where development prospects were inviting. Israel, however, failed to respond to the offer. Za'im's tenure was short-lived; within five months he was overthrown in a military coup.[43]

While extending to Palestinians nearly all the benefits of Syrian citizenship, the government has kept strict control over matters pertaining to the refugees. In 1949 it established the Palestine Arab Refugee Institution (PARI) to manage day-to-day affairs, including registration of births, deaths, marriages, divorces, and property ownership. Since 1949, PARI and its successor organization, the General Authority for Palestine Refugees (GAPAR), have been the dominant authority in the camps and in Syria's Palestinian community. GAPAR, a department of the Ministry of Social Affairs and Labor, closely watches all UNRWA activities and frequently intervenes in the appointment of local UNRWA officials and teachers. GAPAR has its own budget and refugee assistance program but cofinances some programs with UNRWA. On numerous occasions, Syrian security authorities have arrested UNRWA employees and teachers without consultation with or explanation to UNRWA. Syrian government restrictions on and interventions in the Palestinian community are not, however, discriminatory; they reflect the policies of the government toward all inhabitants of the country. Generally speaking, Palestinians in Syria enjoy the same civil rights, or lack thereof, as Syrians.

Palestinians have opened shops, established businesses, and formed companies on their own or in partnership with Syrians. The law does not differentiate between Syrians and non-Syrians except in a few instances: For instance, non-Syrians (including Palestinians) may not buy or acquire land except under special circumstances. There is no discrimination in employment. The law states: "Employed persons who are citizens of any of the nations belonging to the Arab League shall receive equal treatment with Syrian workers in all matters. . . . " In some cases, Palestinians are given preference over other foreigners. The law provides that only Syrian citizens may be employed in the civil service; Palestinians, however, are exempt and "shall be treated on the same footing as Syrians with the right of keeping Palestinian citizenship" when applying for government employment.[44]

Palestinians are more integrated into the country's economic, social, and political life in Syria than in any other Arab country apart from Jordan. They have been prominent in the military and in the leadership of the Ba'ath Party. Syrian authorities have permitted Palestinians to form a number of their own paramilitary and other organizations. Most notable is Sa'iqah, an offshoot of the Vanguards of the Popular War of Liberation. The latter were cadres drawn from the Palestinian branch of the Ba'ath Party, which was based in Damascus.

Separate Palestinian organizations for women, students, labor, youth, and so forth have been permitted, but all are closely monitored by the Syrian Ba'ath leaders, and their policies and pronouncements are always consistent with Syrian policy. In the internecine battles fought among various Palestinian guerrilla factions during the 1980s, President Hafez al-Assad usually backed dissident anti-Arafat groups such as Fatah Uprising, the Popular Front for the Liberation of Palestine (PFLP), the PFLP-General Command, and the Popular Struggle Front.

Despite periodic reconciliations between President Assad and the PLO mainstream led by Arafat, the Syrian government continues its domination over all phases of Palestinian life in Syria, ensuring that they conform with government policies. Given Syria's willingness to accept the Palestinians and offer them treatment nearly equal to that given its own citizens, the problems of future political and economic integration are not as grave in Syria as in other Arab countries. Even Jordan, which has offered full political integration to the refugees, cannot extend the same economic opportunities. However, Syria's willingness to complete the integration of its Palestinian refugees is contingent on a peace settlement with Israel and on Syria's recovery from recent economic setbacks.

Prospects for Solution

Discussions of solutions to the Palestine refugee question have focused on repatriation, compensation, and resettlement. Each of these terms carries great emotional weight; each is seen by one party or another as a code word with far-reaching implications; each represents a policy that will be legally and technically complicated to carry out.

Repatriation

In the early days of the Palestine dispute, *repatriation* meant the return of the refugees to their homes in Israel. Since 1967, the term has also meant a return to some part of Palestine, not necessarily an original home, in the West Bank or Gaza, beyond the 1949 armistice frontiers (the so-called Green Line).

Repatriation is identified with the "right of return"; in the case of Palestine this right derives from UN General Assembly Resolution 194 (III), passed in December 1948 at the third session of the Assembly. The part of the resolution concerning refugees was one of fifteen paragraphs dealing with various aspects of the conflict. Perhaps the most significant provision established the three-member UN Conciliation Commission for Palestine (CCP). The contents of Resolution 194 were adapted from recommendations in the September 1948 progress report of Count Folke Bernadotte, the UN mediator in Palestine.

In addition to making recommendations about borders, internationalization of Jerusalem, recognition of Israel, and measures to establish peace, Bernadotte also stated: "The right of the Arab refugees to return to their homes in Jewish-controlled territory at the earliest possible date should be affirmed by the United Nations, and their repatriation, resettlement and economic and social rehabilitation, and payment of adequate compensation for the property of those choosing not to return, should be supervised and assisted by the United Nations conciliation commission described . . . below."[45]

Although the General Assembly modified and qualified the mediator's recommendations, it accepted them in principle. (See UN General Assembly Resolution 194.) The resolution makes no reference to a right of return per se, nor is there any suggestion that such a right has been generally accepted in international law; the resolution states that refugees "should be permitted" to return. It adds to the mediator's recommendations a provision that returnees should be refugees "wishing to return to their homes and live in peace with their neighbors." Instead of the mediator's "earliest possible date," the General Assembly called for repatriation at "the earliest practicable date." Both proposals called for compensation to "those choosing not to return," and for the CCP to assist or facilitate in refugee "repatriation, resettlement and economic and social rehabilitation." The issue of return was raised again after the 1967 war when the UN Security Council, in Resolution 237, called on Israel "to facilitate the return of those inhabitants who have fled the areas since the outbreak of hostilities."

The question of refugees' right to return to their homes is ambiguous in international law. To the extent that such a right is accepted, it usually applies to refugees returning to states of their original nationality. Since the vast majority of Palestine refugees were never Israeli citizens, this "right" is not generally seen as applicable to them. There is far more emphasis in international codes on not forcing refugees to return to countries from which they have fled.

Early attempts to resolve the Palestine problem included American pressure on Israel to accept the return of a substantial number of refugees. In 1949, President Truman urged the return of between 200,000 and 300,000. Israel responded by offering to accept refugees from the Gaza Strip, provided Israel was given sovereignty over the area. Also in 1949, Israel offered to accept 100,000 refugees provided the government could settle them where settlement best fit plans for economic development. Neither offer was accepted by the United States or any Arab government at that time.

The reuniting of families has been permitted on an individual, case-by-case basis. Before 1967, Israel authorized the return of some 40,500 refugees to families within its borders. After the 1967 war, another 60,000 were permitted to return to the West Bank and 10,000 to Jerusalem. However, the return of these refugees was perceived by Israel not as a refugee right, but as a humanitarian gesture on the part of Israel.[46]

The issue received a great deal of attention prior to the 1992 Ottawa meeting on refugees when a U.S. State Department spokeswoman stated at a press briefing that her government continued to support Resolution 194. However, the United States urged Palestinian delegates at the Ottawa conference not to raise the issue of return at such an early phase of the peace negotiations lest it disrupt the proceedings.

David Levy, Israel's foreign minister, and Zalman Shoval, its ambassador to Washington, maintained that American officials privately assured them the United States did not support a Palestinian right of return. In the past, the United States had voted against other resolutions endorsing this return as a right. The position was reinforced in a secret letter sent by President Richard Nixon to Prime Minister Golda Meir in 1971, in which he stated: "We [the United States] shall not press Israel to accept a solution to the problem of the refugees which will basically alter the Jewish character of the State of Israel and endanger its security." The letter was supposedly part of the Nixon administration's effort to broker an end to the 1970 War of Attrition.[47]

The Arab attitude toward Resolution 194 has been ambiguous. Initially, the Arab states voted against the resolution because it implied recognition of Israel, but by 1949, several Arab states supported it. The Palestinian delegation at the UN opposed the resolution, maintaining that Israel had no legal right to prevent a return of the "indigenous population" to their homes; this was a right that did not

require further international approval. Nevertheless, the refugees
have always regarded Resolution 194 as an affirmation of their right
to return to their homes. Several UNRWA directors have reported
that "the refugees as a whole insist upon the choice provided for
them in the General Assembly Resolution 194 (III), that is, repatriation or compensation. In the absence of that choice, they bitterly
oppose anything which has even the semblance of a permanent settlement elsewhere."[48]

The right of return cannot easily be discarded by Palestinians.
Since 1948, it has acquired emotional connotations of such significance that the term became the basis of Palestinian nationalism in
much the same way that the return to *Eretz Israel* became the foundation of Zionism. The concept of return permeates modern Palestinian literature; it is at the core of history taught to children in
refugee camps throughout the region, and is usually the first thought
expressed by average Palestinians when discussing Middle East problems. To many, the right of return is an important symbol; recognition would remove the stigma of second-class citizenship imposed on
Palestinians, a stigma that exists even in Jordan, where by law the
refugees have equal rights.

While realizing that refugee return to Israel within the 1949
armistice lines is neither feasible nor practical, many who emphasize
the demand insist that Palestinians at least be given the right of return
to the territory occupied by Israel in 1967. It is acknowledgment of
the right, rather than its implementation, that is demanded.

Ordinary Palestinians are skeptical of "rational" arguments based
on the limitations of economic absorptive capacity or the fact that
refugees' homes and villages no longer exist. In their view, if Israel
could bring more than a quarter of a million Russian Jews into the
country during the last year or two, it should be possible for an equal
number of Palestinians to return to Israel. If funds can be obtained to
build homes and provide for tens of thousands of Jews from Europe
and Ethiopia, money can be found for Palestinian repatriation. While
Palestinian political leaders and intellectuals may comprehend the
subtleties in the differences between Jewish immigration to Israel and
refugees' return to Palestine, pushing these arguments too far with

the man in the street is likely to provoke acrimonious accusations of pro-Zionist sympathies.

To most Israelis, the "right of return" for Palestine refugees is perceived as a code term for undermining the existence of the Jewish state. If it is accepted as a general principle, a right that Palestinians are free to exercise or not, Israelis fear the influx of enough Palestinians to alter the country's demography. The return of large numbers of Palestinians could, some say, lead to "Lebanonization" of Israel, resulting in a violent struggle between ethnic groups. Arab assertions that such an influx is unlikely and that the right of return will be recognized only as a principle does not reassure many Israelis, even among those in the peace camp.

Among well-informed Palestinians, who are aware that conditions have so changed since 1948 that an actual return to original homes is no longer possible, the slogan is interpreted in diverse ways. Some envisage the return of a small number of Palestinians to their native villages and towns. Others see a return to some small enclave within Israel's borders near to or adjoining a previous residence. For some, a return to Palestine does not necessarily mean a return to Israel, but to a part of the country outside the Green Line. This more limited concept is implicit in the Palestinian Declaration of Independence and the PNC's political communiqué issued at Algiers on November 15, 1988. While both documents refer to the right of return, they also recognize a two-state (Palestine and Israel) solution to the conflict.[49] The question inherent in discussion of the issue is, Return to where? What concerns Israelis is that when most refugees discuss return, they perceive it as a return to pre-1948 Palestine, not to Israel. Therefore, even acceptance of the principle carries the implied threat of Israel's demise. Since there are no definitive, internationally recognized borders for either Israel or a Palestine entity, it is unclear whether return means a return to Israel or to Palestine. The 1968 PLO National Covenant states: "Palestine, within the frontiers that existed under the British mandate, is an indivisible territorial unit" (Article 2).[50] However, since the November 1988 meeting of the PNC, the organization's mainstream has accepted division of mandatory Palestine into Israel and a Palestinian state with the 1949 armistice lines as the approximate boundary, the final border to be determined in peace negotiations.

The other side of the coin is that denial of the right of return to Palestinians is discriminatory because the right is enshrined for Jews in the Israeli Law of Return. Withholding the right from Palestinians connotes denial of their right to a homeland. According to Rashid Khalidi, the Palestinians have accepted "certain crucial limitations" on the absolute right of return. These include accepting the principle that refugees "choosing not to return" are eligible for compensation for property left in Israel. This option, seen in the past as selling out, has now been validated by the PLO; implicit in its acceptance is recognition of Israel's existence.[51]

The Palestinian mainstream, Khalidi maintains, accepts that returnees must agree "to live at peace with their neighbors," also implying recognition of Israel and the obligation of returnees to accept Israeli law and authority. A third implicit limitation is that there is no specific mention of where returnees might be settled, either within Israel or in the rest of Palestine; however, the recognition that refugees will not necessarily return to their original homes is implicit.

Given the nearly unanimous opposition of all Zionist political parties in Israel to the recognition of a Palestinian Arab right of return, extensive repatriation does not seem to be a viable option. Since the Arab exodus from Israeli-held territory in 1947–48, nearly all of the property formerly owned by Palestinian Arabs has been absorbed into the country's economy through an elaborate and complicated legal process. Most Palestinian towns and villages in pre-1948 mandatory Palestine have disappeared, been taken over by new settlers, or otherwise lost their Arab identity. Not only would it be difficult to reestablish these former Arab sites, it is unlikely that any Israeli government would sanction such measures. As long as Israel's guiding ideology is Zionist, public opinion will not allow any government to adopt measures that substantially increase the ratio of Arab to Jewish citizens within the Green Line. (The present balance is approximately 82 percent Jewish and 18 percent Arab, with a continuing increase in favor of the Arab population.)

Several Israeli demographers have cautioned that before the end of the next century, because of higher birth rates, the country's Arab population will nearly equal its Jewish population. Therefore, the greatest concession Israel is likely to make is to authorize a small-scale family-reunion project in which a token number of Palestinian refugees would be permitted to return to existing Israeli Arab settlements. However, no Israeli government will accept that this return is a "right."

Return to a Palestinian State

Although implementation of the right of return to Israel within the Green Line on any significant scale is unlikely, it is politically feasible that over an extended period a substantial number of refugees could "return" to territory within a new Palestinian political entity. This form of return would combine repatriation in its broadest sense with resettlement in new homes; compensation would play a major role in helping to implement this kind of repatriation-resettlement.

The economic problems to be confronted are as important as the political difficulties in establishing a Palestinian entity. Even if the political issues (borders, form of government, relationships to Israel and Jordan) were resolved, the economic problems would be momentous. One of the principal arguments against the establishment of so small an independent entity (the West Bank comprises 2,270 square miles; Gaza, 140 square miles) is that it would not be economically viable, although today several UN member states are smaller in area and population and have fewer resources.

A major difficulty is how to define economic viability. There is no definition commonly accepted by social scientists. If independence from foreign aid were used as a criterion, few developing countries would fit the definition; it certainly would not apply to Israel. Some economists claim that the term implies rapid growth of production and income, reduced unemployment, and decline of budgetary deficits. Again, few Third World countries would meet these qualifications. According to an early economic study of the West Bank, "[a] country will be regarded as economically viable if its economic characteristics permit it to experience sustained economic growth and rising welfare per capita and if its economic processes function well enough to permit a modicum of social and political stability; conversely, economic viability requires political and economic conditions that permit growth and development."[52]

Brian Van Arkadie, who has also discussed this issue at length, observes:

> "Could a West Bank–Gaza Strip state be viable?" is . . . the wrong question. For this, as for other territory about which the question might be asked, the answer is neither "Yes" nor "No." The only realistic answer is "Only if . . . ." Very few economies could be successful in theory under conditions of autarky. Virtually none are in practice. . . . Many economies exist which, on a priori reasoning, might seem economically implausible, that is, unable to provide their populations with a satisfactory livelihood. Some of these survive without much success; others do well under extraordinarily adverse conditions.[53]

Questions have been raised about whether a credible process of economic development can be initiated before a peace settlement is reached, with the West Bank and Gaza still under Israeli rule. The experience of the first 25 years of Israeli occupation under Labor, Likud, and National Unity governments indicates that such development is unlikely. Even after a peace settlement, major problems would be encountered in reversing the economic effects of the first quarter-century of occupation, when the economies of the territories were made ancillary to Israel's economy. During that era, economic activity in the territories was subject to the needs of the occupying power. The road network was planned, expanded, and integrated with Israel's roads; the electricity grid became part of the overall Israeli system; priority in water use and development was given to Israeli needs; agriculture, industry, trade, and commerce were allowed to develop only within a larger scheme according to Israeli plans. Even the Palestinian labor force in the territories became so tied to Israel's economy that it will be no easy task to sever its links with the occupiers.[54]

At present, a large percentage of Arabs in the Occupied Territories, both those in camps and elsewhere, work in Israel, although the

number has been reduced by about half since the Gulf War and the
influx of Russian Jews. These developments have caused widespread
joblessness in Gaza and the West Bank. Estimates of unemployment
in the territories are as high as 50 percent. The economic impact of
the Gulf War has created a severe crisis that is unlikely to diminish
before substantial progress is made in the peace negotiations. The
situation has been further exacerbated by Israel's closing its borders
to West Bank and Gaza Arabs following terrorist attacks on civilians
within the Green Line.

As a result of the war and declining economic conditions in Israel
and the surrounding countries, various forms of direct and indirect
economic assistance have ended. Assistance to Palestinian institutions from several Arab countries has stopped. Remittances sent from
relatives working in the Gulf have come to a halt. Trade between the
territories and surrounding Arab countries has declined. Many home
workshops in the territories that provided piecework on contract to
Israeli establishments have been cut off from contacts across the
Green Line.

From the beginning of the occupation in 1967, Israeli authorities
have done little to develop the economy of the West Bank and Gaza.
True, material conditions greatly improved for many after 1967. The
education system was expanded; health facilities and conditions improved; inhabitants acquired many more material possessions, such
as automobiles, televisions, refrigerators, and other household con-
veniences. Construction of middle- and upper-class housing was
extensive. Many of these benefits were the result of income earned
by Palestinians employed in Israel. Little, however, was done to
expand or improve the indigenous economy. A UN official reported
in 1991 that "Israel's long-term policy of suppressing large-scale
commercial activity in the Occupied Territory has resulted in a weak
economy, with a limited manufacturing sector largely dependent
upon Israel." Palestinian industry operated in a captive market domi-
nated by Israeli industrial products.[55]

Israeli authorities made little effort "to encourage further agricultural development through basic structural changes such as investment in infrastructure, extension of irrigation systems, or land

reform," and Palestinian agriculture was "allowed to develop only insofar as it would not affect Israeli agriculture, and on condition that its development would not involve a fiscal or economic drain on the Israeli economy or government."[56]

Palestinian farms received little in the way of protection or subsidies. Overall investment opportunities were limited to those complementing the better organized and richer Israeli economy. As Van Arkadie observed, the poorer economy was unable to "use traditional policy instruments such as tariffs or exchange rate adjustments to serve their own economic objectives. Unable to modify public policy decisions or the market process in order to meet local needs, the West Bank and the Gaza Strip economies have been affected by Israeli tariffs, exchange rate adjustments, and fiscal and monetary policy necessarily framed to meet the needs of the Israeli economy."[57]

By the end of 1991, a UN official reported:

> The West Bank is on the verge of economic collapse as it faces its most serious recession since 1967. UNRWA and other relief organizations working in the area do not have the resources or the authority to make the necessary changes and to establish the infrastructure essential to placing the economy of the West Bank on a sound footing. Unless the situation improves within the next six months, the economy will be moribund and Palestinians, already selling their goods as savings run out, will be facing impoverishment.[58]

Prospects for major improvement of the economy in the Occupied Territories are not bright, especially considering the difficult problems facing Israel during the next decade. One of the most daunting Israeli priorities at present is to absorb about one million new Russian Jewish immigrants by the end of the decade. Neither Israel nor its supporters abroad are likely to make the investments necessary to improve the Palestinian economy.

Among the first problems to confront a Palestine entity is the large number of refugees already within its borders. They now constitute approximately half the total population in the West Bank and Gaza. More than a fifth of the two-million-plus people in the prospective Palestinian state still live in UNRWA camps. Before the entity could admit large numbers of additional refugees, it would have to begin to absorb the 450,000 camp inhabitants now within its borders.

Another major obstacle is the 245,000 Jewish settlers established in some 250 East Jerusalem, West Bank, and Gaza locales since 1967. These settlers now constitute approximately 13 percent of the population in the Occupied Territories.[59] Although it would not be difficult to relocate many of these settlements, several have developed into sizable urban centers whose inhabitants will not willingly leave.

Despite these difficulties, several optimistic studies have been made that postulate an economically viable sovereign or autonomous Palestine within a decade after independence. These studies envisage the absorption of the million refugees now living in the territories (over 450,000 in camps) as well as the integration of several hundred thousand additional Palestinians, with priority given to those now in camps located in Lebanon, Syria, and Jordan.

UNRWA and Palestinian grassroots organizations, many of them established before the occupation, can provide a core of skilled personnel to initiate a new development program. Many of these groups have expanded their development activities since 1967 in areas including health, education, agriculture, land reclamation, and women's activities. "Local councils, charitable societies, professional associations, voluntary committees, [and] production cooperatives—now numbering over 400 and found in virtually all Palestinian towns, villages and camps—sprang up, especially in the past decade, in part to fill a widening gap in officially supplied services."[60] Many of these activities intensified during the Intifada, and a new type of organization, the "popular committee," was added to the existing infrastructure. The Palestinian national movement's previous neglect of traditional differences between urban and rural communities was also overcome during the uprising.

Palestinian economists believe that once freed from the restraints of occupation, these organizations can make great strides. Among recent studies and analyses of Palestinian economic potential are George T. Abed's *The Economic Viability of a Palestinian State* and *Masterplanning: The State of Palestine, Suggested Guidelines*, prepared for American Near East Refugee Aid (ANERA) by the Center for

Engineering and Planning in Ramallah, West Bank. Both studies postulate an independent Palestinian state free to determine its own economic policies and plans. Both assume total Israeli withdrawal, including surrender of control over land and water resources, departure of Jewish settlers who refuse to become Palestinian citizens, and severance of the network of economic ties that Israel has imposed during the past quarter-century. Both assume an overland link between Gaza and the West Bank.

Abed focuses on the initial reconstruction of the infrastructure with public financing at first, then external aid, and private-sector involvement at a later date. Compensation to be paid for property left in Israel in 1947–48 is seen by most Palestinians as one of the major sources of financing for development.

Abed envisages the return of nearly 750,000 Palestinians to the West Bank within the first two to three years of independence. Preference would be given to those living in refugee camps in Jordan, Syria, and Lebanon, who would "seek to return almost immediately within the framework of a phased repatriation program."[61] These refugees would be added to the more than 450,000 camp occupants presently living in the territories.

Abed also revives the 1949 U.S. and Israeli proposals to return 50,000 to 100,000 people "to areas conquered by Israel in 1948" (that is, within the 1949 armistice frontiers).[62] Migration would bring the total population of Palestine to 3.3 million by the year 2000. The figure 750,000 is based on giving priority to refugee camp inhabitants plus an arbitrary chosen ratio of 20 percent for refugees living outside camps in the three Arab host countries. An additional 30,000 to 50,000 Palestinians from other countries who "for various reasons have residency difficulties" would be repatriated.[63]

These demographic postulates suggest that the population density for the whole state would reach the rather high figure of 560 persons per square kilometer by the year 2000. Gaza's density would exceed 2,700 per square kilometer. These figures, although high, do not seem unworkable: Israel has a population density of 210 persons per square kilometer; Belgium, 325; Japan, 325; the Netherlands, 360; Taiwan, 555; Hong Kong, 1,900; and Singapore, 4,200.[64]

Masterplanning envisages the return of some 750,000 Palestinians during the first five years of independence and another 750,000 in the following five years. Returnees would be resettled in existing urban and rural towns as well as in new ones to be constructed at selected sites.[65] From a base population of 2.265 million in 1990, the study projects a total of 4.8 million persons living in independent Palestine by the year 2000; 1.5 million would be returnees, most of them probably refugees. Given an average family of six persons, there will be between 800,000 and 810,000 households. The increases in population density per square kilometer between 1990 and 2000 in the four districts of the projected state would be as follows: Nablus, 268 to 595; Jerusalem (Arabic, al-Quds), 277 to 658; Hebron (Arabic, al-Khalil), 222 to 697; Gaza, 2,122 to 3,322.[66]

Can an independent Palestinian entity sustain a population between 3.3 and 4.8 million people? These two studies as well as research by other economists assume that the country, with its limited resources but with a highly skilled labor force, can become relatively viable with radical economic reconstruction and reorientation. The basic infrastructure (road network, transportation, housing facilities, education system, electricity grid, and water sources) needs to be redirected from its present orientation toward meeting Israel's needs to the requirements of an independent Palestine. Productive capacity in agriculture, industry, and services must be greatly increased through substantial investments in modernization.

Although the Palestinian community is one of the most educated in the Middle East, a Palestinian state would nevertheless require major programs to develop high-level technical, scientific, and administrative skills. In 1991, UNRWA decided to initiate a new income-generating program; one of its objectives was to stimulate private initiative because "in the Palestinian economies there is, particularly in the Occupied Territory, a lack of general entrepreneurial and labor-management skills. . . ."[67]

The development program outlined by Abed "would not only lay the foundations for sustained economic growth, it would also help create job opportunities for an estimated 140,000 workers among the returnees as well as for reabsorption of large numbers of Palestinians now employed in Israel, in addition to a general upgrading of jobs currently held by the 155,000 workers employed in the local economy in the West Bank and Gaza."[68]

Masterplanning estimates a total demand for 1.25 million jobs, accounting for 25 percent of the population, by 2000. This estimate is based on natural population increases and the return of 1.5 million Palestinians. The drafters did not believe that all workers would be able to find employment in Palestine; therefore, "it is expected that serious efforts will have to be made in order to arrange for the absorption of the work-force surplus in the neighboring and regional markets under favorable working conditions."[69]

Abed estimates that the total cost of the infrastructural program for a Palestinian state during the next 10 to 12 years would be some $13 billion at 1990 prices (table 6). This amount would include funds raised in both the public and private sectors. The most costly item would be housing. Some 200,000 units would have to be built merely to house the refugees now living in the West Bank and Gaza. This housing would provide space for some 1.2 million additional people (based on six persons per unit).

Housing construction would employ 25,000 workers annually, although initially as many as 40,000 might be needed. In addition to providing new housing for refugees, it would be necessary to alleviate already existing overcrowding and deterioration of the present housing stock. With the return of several hundred thousand refugees and other Palestinians, it would be necessary to more than double Abed's figure of $13 billion. To meet this demand, construction would have to increase to about ten times the present annual production level. "The estimated demand would overwhelm the existing institutional and financial capacities, and would require an intensive upgrading of the administrative, managerial and technical capability of the local authorities in order to increase their capacity to plan, implement and administer housing projects."[70]

Abed estimates that in addition to the cost of revitalizing the infrastructure, another $12 billion will be required for private-sector development of industry, agriculture, and services such as tourism and banking. Funding would come from diverse sources: about

Table 6. The State of Palestine: Estimates of Infrastructural Costs of a Reconstruction and Development Program (in Millions of Dollars at 1990 Prices).

A. Physical infrastructure	9,500
1. Housing (200,000 units)	4,500
2. Roads (5,000 km)	1,250
3. Irrigation, land reclamation, and rural infrastructure	1,200
4. Power/electricity capacity and networks	750
5. Water and sewage facilities	600
6. Communications	400
7. Air and seaport facilities	350
8. Public buildings	300
9. Other facilities	150
B. Social infrastructure	2,450
10. Hospitals and other facilities	1,200
11. Educational facilities	600
12. Social institutions	300
13. Public facilities (parks, etc.)	150
14. Tourism facilities (public share)	100
15. Other facilities	100
Subtotal (A+B)	11,950
C. Contingency (10%)	1,200
D. Total (A+B+C)	13,150

Source: George T. Abed, *The Economic Viability of a Palestinian State* (Washington, D.C.: Institute for Palestine Studies, 1990), 25.

$6 billion from Arab countries, $4 billion from bilateral assistance, and $2 billion from international financial and development institutions. Private-sector funding would come largely from Palestinian, Arab, and international business interests investing in projects from which they expect to profit.

A considerably lower estimate of the costs of reviving the economy of a Palestinian entity in the West Bank and Gaza is provided by a September 1993 World Bank assessment ("Developing the Occupied Territories"). According to the bank's conservative analysis, high priority investments in the public sector over the next 10 years should be about $3 billion. The initial focus of public investment would be to upgrade water supplies, sewage plants, solid waste disposal, the road system, electricity grids, and education and health facilities.

Private capital investment of $2.5 billion would also be required over the next 10 years, much of it to come from prosperous Palestinians abroad. It should be noted, however, that these calculations are based on requirements for the existing population in the West Bank and Gaza and do not take into consideration the return of large numbers of refugees or other Palestinians.

The five-year interim agreement signed between Israel and the PLO in September 1993 includes a protocol calling for establishment of an Israeli-Palestinian Continuing Committee for Economic Cooperation to deal with matters such as water resources, electricity production, energy development, transport and communications, trade and industry, human resources, and finance. Another protocol states that the two sides will cooperate in raising funds for these projects from the Group of Seven industrialized nations, the Organization for Economic Cooperation and Development, regional Arab institutions, and private sources.

Soon after the Israeli-PLO agreement was signed, an international donors conference attended by 43 countries pledged $2 billion in assistance over five years, including $600 million from the European Community and $500 million from the United States (*Washington Post*, October 2, 1993).

Another source of anticipated funding is compensation to be paid for Palestinian property abandoned in Israel. One form of compensation might be buildings constructed by Jewish settlers in the more than 100 settlements completed since 1967. *Masterplanning* estimates that these settlements contain between 50,000 and 70,000 housing units that could be integrated into the housing stock of Palestinian towns and villages after Jewish settlers depart.[71] Housing in some of the more remote Jewish settlements might also provide space for returning Palestinians. Since 1967, several billion dollars worth of housing and infrastructure construction has been completed in West Bank and Gaza Jewish settlements. Much investment has been disguised in Israeli budget items; thus no precise figure is available for the overall value of Jewish investment in the territories.

Estimates of Israeli investment in Jewish settlements are complicated by the issue of Jerusalem, where the great majority of housing has been constructed. Since 1967, Israel has extended the borders of Jerusalem far beyond those of the mandatory capital to include large tracts of land and several villages in the former Jordanian West Bank. Therefore, the Jerusalem question cannot be separated from other issues involving refugee settlement, such as borders between Israel and the Palestinian entity, compensation, resettlement, and repatriation. Recent estimates place the Jewish population of the West Bank in areas beyond present-day municipal Jerusalem at about 125,000; the Jewish population of Arab East Jerusalem and West Bank areas annexed to the Jerusalem municipalities is about 129,000 in 12 Jewish neighborhoods.[72]

Israeli expenditures beyond the Green Line during 1992 have been projected at $1.2 billion; the amount in 1991 was $2 billion. Thus, total investment in areas added to Israel since 1967 must reach several tens of billions of dollars. A critical problem in resolving the compensation issue will be to balance the value of Arab property left in Israel against Israeli investment in West Bank and Gaza Jewish settlements, including housing stock and infrastructure that can be used by a Palestine state. In addition, some Israelis, especially many who immigrated from Middle Eastern countries, demand that property left by Jewish communities in Arab countries be included in the compensation equation.

Compensation

The issue of compensation for property left in Israel by Arab refugees also derives from the recommendations of UN mediator Count Folke Bernadotte and UN Resolution 194 (III). The resolution called for two types of compensation: to refugees "choosing not to return" to their homes in Israel, and "for loss of or damage to property which under principles of international law or equity should be made good by the Governments or authorities responsible." In the more than forty years that have passed since these recommendations were proposed, the issue has been periodically debated, but little if any progress has been made to resolve it.

The problem of compensation has become much more complicated because property that was abandoned in 1947–48 has become

increasingly difficult to identify and evaluate. Since most Arab property was absorbed into Israel's economy, it has been transformed,
often beyond recognition. In many cases it has passed through several
successive owners and has been classified and reclassified under a
variety of Israeli laws. Much land that was once agricultural has
become urban; in many cases where there were once Palestinian Arab
farms, orchards, or orange groves, there are now Jewish high-rise
apartment or office buildings. Movable property, such as vehicles,
factory machinery, household goods, farm animals, and personal possessions, has long since disappeared without any record.

Property values have increased substantially in the past 40 years;
it would be difficult if not impossible to estimate the value of property
in a modern urban center today relative to its value as farmland two
generations ago. Many former Arab buildings (homes, offices, workshops, public structures) that still exist have been reconstructed so
that their worth today has little relationship to market costs in
1947–48. Furthermore, persons who had owned property in mandatory Palestine would now often be difficult to locate.

However, these problems do not vitiate the rights of those who
lost property as a result of the 1948 conflict to obtain some form of
compensation. Precedents exist in similar situations for compensation to war victims many years after they lost their property.
They include the Turkish agreement to compensate Armenian
refugees in the 1920 Treaty of Sèvres, a 1930 agreement between
Hungary and Romania, a 1948 agreement between India and Pakistan, and the 1952 Luxembourg agreement between the Federal
Republic of Germany and Israel for payment of reparations to
Jewish refugees.

One of the first tasks of CCP was to identify and evaluate Arab
property abandoned in Israel. The CCP Refugee Office estimated
that more than 80 percent of Israel's total area of 20,850 square
kilometers represented abandoned Arab lands, although only a little
more than a quarter was considered cultivable. Three-quarters of former Arab lands were classified as submarginal or semidesert; most of
these were in the Negev. Most of the Negev land, constituting
about half the area of Israel, was occupied by nomad tribes whose

ownership was not clearly defined. During the mandate, tribal rights were not challenged, although actual title as state domain by the government was "presumed." The status of these lands was ambiguous, because it was not possible to assume with certainty that they were part of the state domain. These estimates of CCP were based on figures in *Village Statistics* published by the former mandatory government.

Perhaps more significant than this global estimate is the fact that between 1948 and 1953, 350 of the 370 new Jewish settlements established in Israel were on former Arab property (absentee property). By 1954, more than one-third of the Jewish population lived on former Arab land, and an additional 250,000 Israeli Jews, including one-third of the new immigrants, lived in abandoned Arab urban property. Whole cities, such as Jaffa, Acre, Lydda, Ramleh, Beit Shan, and Migdal-Gad, plus some 400 towns and villages and large parts of 94 others, were abandoned by Palestinian Arab refugees. These areas contained nearly a quarter of all buildings in Israel at the time. Most of the 120,000 *dunums* (a *dunum* is about a quarter of an acre) of Arab orange groves, about half the citrus land in Palestine at the end of the mandate, were taken over by the Israeli government. In addition to the large citrus areas, 40,000 *dunums* of vineyards, at least 10,000 *dunums* of other orchards, and nearly 95 percent of Israel's olive groves were abandoned by the refugees. CCP estimated that the amount of Israel's cultivable abandoned Arab land was nearly two and one-half times the total area of Jewish-owned property at the end of the mandate.[73]

These figures underscore the importance of abandoned Arab property in facilitating the absorption of 720,000 new Jewish immigrants into the Israeli economy during the first five years of independence. Palestinian economists estimate that during a similar five- to ten-year period, the new Palestinian state could absorb approximately the same number of refugees, and property left by Israeli settlers in the West Bank and Gaza would have a role similar to that of Palestinian Arab refugee property abandoned in Israel.

In 1950, when the UN General Assembly passed a resolution noting "with concern" that compensation had not yet been paid, it called on CCP to establish a refugee office to "make such arrangements as it may consider necessary for the assessment and payment of compensation" (394[V]). A committee of experts on compensation was attached to the refugee office and given the task of setting a global evaluation of abandoned Arab property. CCP's estimate was based on evaluation of property within the 1949 armistice frontiers, the unofficial borders of Israel until 1967. The value of land was determined by crop productivity in rural areas and by rents in urban areas, based on values and condition of property on November 29, 1947, the date of the UN Partition Resolution and the beginning of the civil war within Palestine. No value was placed on uncultivable land.

In calculating the worth of movable property, including industrial equipment, commercial stocks, motor vehicles, household effects, agricultural equipment, and livestock, the proportion of values in the case of Turks leaving Greece and Greeks leaving Turkey after World War I was used because of the similarity between these communities and the Palestinian Arab rural and urban communities.[74]

The figures represented an estimate of total wealth in the Palestinian Arab community in November 1947. The amount belonging to refugees was estimated at about three-quarters of the total. The Palestine pound (LP) was then equal to one pound sterling; the total value of abandoned Arab property was estimated at approximately 120 million pounds sterling (at 1947 rates), or approximately 1.85 billion 1990 U.S. dollars.

In 1949–50, Israel agreed in principle to pay compensation but with several qualifications: Compensation payments would be part of an overall peace settlement—rather than individual compensation, payment would be a global sum contributed to a UN fund for resettling Arab refugees; the loss of Jewish property in areas of Palestine occupied by Arab forces had to be taken into account; Israeli claims against the Arab states for war damages would have to be considered. Israel's offer was weakened by the exodus of more than 100,000 Jews from Iraq in 1951 when demands were made to balance the Palestinian Arab refugee account against Iraqi Jewish property.

By the end of the Suez-Sinai war in 1956, the compensation issue had all but disappeared from Israel's agenda. As a result of the war,

Jewish property sequestered by the Egyptian government also became part of the equation; there was strong public sentiment against payment of compensation to the Arab refugees. In 1954, leaders of the Iraqi Jewish community in Israel estimated that the value of the community's abandoned property was 156 million Israeli pounds, approximately the value the CCP Refugee Office placed on abandoned Palestinian Arab property.

Counterclaims by Jews from the Middle East were strengthened in 1974 with the formation of the World Organization of Jews from Arab Countries (WOJAC) under the leadership of deputy Knesset speaker Mordechai Ben-Porat, a prominent Iraqi-Jewish personality in the Labor Alignment. WOJAC, in its attempts to rally Jews from the Arab world into a powerful bloc, received quasi-official status and funds from the Jewish Agency, an international organization that is recognized by the Israeli government and was formed to further Zionist goals. WOJAC claimed that more than 800,000 Jews were refugees from Arab countries and that they and their descendants constituted nearly half of the Jewish population of Israel. According to Ben-Porat, "the Jews left about five times more property behind in Arab countries than the Arabs left behind here [in Israel]." When Iraq, Libya, Yemen, Egypt, and Syria invited all Jews who left after 1948 to return, reclaim their property, and renew their residence, WOJAC dismissed the offer as a "return [to the] gallows or to prison."[75]

Israel maintained throughout the discussions that its obligation was to the UN rather than to the Arab states or the Palestinian community and that willingness to pay compensation in no way constituted acceptance of responsibility for the refugee flight or for the war that led to it. Agreement to pay would "have to put an end to the whole problem of the Arab refugees in all its aspects, both humanitarian and material, so far as the State of Israel is concerned."[76]

By 1957, Israel linked the problem of compensation to the Arab blockade and boycott of Israeli goods. At the UN, Israel's ambassador warned: "It could hardly be practicable for Israel to pump vast sums of money into the economies of neighboring countries, while those countries were trying to bring about Israel's collapse through economic strangulation. It is the policies of the Arab governments which are holding up compensation for the refugees in those countries."[77]

The Arab position since 1948 has been consistent. Israel bears primary responsibility for the refugee flight and for payment to individuals. Compensation should be "an individual right of the refugees personally or of their beneficiaries," and they should be able to exercise it "without any limitations of time or space." To establish any relationship between Israel's financial capabilities and its obligations to pay would be "pure and simple confiscation of the property of the Arab refugee. . . . To restrict this right or to make the payment of compensation dependent on the financial capacity of Israel would be to make this right an illusion and to make Israel a present of the refugees' property." Because of the UN's role in the establishment of Israel, it too has an obligation. "It is only fair that it should pay compensation to the refugees when the principal debtor is insolvent. The UN has, so to speak, taken upon itself this obligation because of its role in the establishment of the new state."[78]

When the Federal Republic of Germany agreed to pay reparations to Israel, the Arab League unsuccessfully attempted to force payment of Arab refugee compensation from the funds Israel was to receive, but both Germany and Israel resisted. Arab authorities in 1951 estimated the "true value" of abandoned property in Israel at LP 2 billion (approximately 36 billion in 1990 U.S. dollars), nearly twenty times the appraisal of CCP's Refugee Office.[79]

Arab economists have disputed the CCP evaluation. They maintain that it was much too low and failed to consider a number of critical items, such as psychological and human suffering, lost opportunity, and public property. Furthermore, they argue, CCP's evaluation did not account for the potential development value of land and placed no value on uncultivable areas.

An evaluation of Arab property in Israel by Yusif A. Sayegh in *The Israeli Economy*, published in 1966 and cited by Sami Hadawi below, offered an estimate of LP 756.7 million at 1947 prices, about halfway between the CCP figure of LP 120 million and the Arab League's LP 2 billion. Hadawi, a former official of the mandatory government who worked with CCP, estimated the value of abandoned Arab property at LP 743,050,000 at 1948 rates. However, when he added human capital losses, the total rose to LP 1,182,200,000. This figure at post-1990 rates would come to well over 25 billion 1990 U.S. dollars.[80]

CCP was never formally or officially dissolved; however, after 1957 it maintained only a shadowy existence. Its records are still intact at UN headquarters in New York, awaiting renewed attempts to resolve the issue of abandoned property and compensation. By the end of 1957, CCP did accomplish three steps toward resolution of the compensation issue: (1) it completed a global estimate of the value of Arab abandoned property; (2) it obtained the release of Arab refugee accounts worth almost LP 4 million that had been frozen in Israeli banks; and (3) it identified individual refugee property holdings abandoned in Israel that were worth a large amount.

Given the many political problems and technical pitfalls surrounding the issue of compensation, it seems unlikely that payments will be settled with individual claimants in an overall settlement. Among the many obstacles to identification of individual claims is the fact that most of the original land registration records in Palestine were destroyed during the 1947–48 fighting or are missing for other reasons. Numerous records were microfilmed and brought to England, but many of these documents were found to be illegible.

The character of the land system in Palestine presents another problem. Most of the country's 16,324,000 *dunums* of abandoned land, including much of the 4,574,000 *dunums* considered cultivable, were never identified by cadastral survey under the mandatory government's Land Settlement Ordinance. Much land was registered under the old Ottoman system, in which parcels of land were identified according to boundaries, without reference to a survey. Entries in the official Register of Deeds could rarely be matched to the parcels to which they purported to refer. Many transactions were private deals concluded outside the Land Registry Offices, and title deeds were not recorded. Nor were successions, which divided land into small pieces, routinely recorded. Therefore, the Register of Deeds, particularly in rural areas, often failed to show true ownership. By the end of the mandate, less than a third of the land was registered under the Land Settlement Ordinance of 1928, which provided for accurately defined parcels based on surveyors' maps.[81]

Most Jewish-owned land was in the "settled" area, but large tracts that became absentee property in Western Galilee, the Jerusalem corridor, and the regions surrounding Safad, Acre, and the Little Triangle were never registered under the Land Settlement Ordinance. Computation of compensation payments for these lands on an individual basis would raise a host of legal and technical difficulties requiring years of investigation and arbitration. It would be extremely difficult to determine the shares of individual village inhabitants because much village land was held collectively in undivided ownership (*musha*). Many of these areas were already in dispute, some with as many as 30 claims per parcel. According to some estimates, 50 to 60 percent of abandoned Arab land was commonly held under the *musha* system.

When compensation does become an agenda item in the negotiations dealing with the refugees, it seems that the most feasible solution will be a trade-off based on the current de facto situation. For example, former Jewish property now in Arab areas such as Iraq, Egypt, and the future Palestine entity will become the property of each Arab party to the conflict, and former Arab property in Israel will retain the status it has acquired since 1948. Thus compensation is unlikely to consist of large amounts of cash or promissory obligations that can be used for development. Rather, it will be in the form of property that has already been absorbed into the economy of the host countries, such as Jewish housing in Damascus that has been taken over by Palestinians, property in Baghdad that is now owned by the government or Iraqi citizens, and property left by Jewish settlers in the West Bank and Gaza that will become part of the infrastructure and housing stock of the Palestine entity.

Resettlement

Although resettlement linked with economic and social rehabilitation of the refugees was an integral part of Resolution 194, the term resettlement always had invidious connotations for the refugees. For most, it meant abandonment of the right of return; therefore, those dealing with the refugees had to be aware of the refugees' extreme sensitivity to the term. During the 1950s, any hint by UNRWA that it was seriously considering "resettlement" as an option often led to violent refugee reactions. When the transfer of refugees from tents to semipermanent shelters began, many rebelled; they refused to leave the tents for fear that they would never return to Palestine. Later, when the semipermanent shelters were replaced with more enduring housing, many again objected. However, in the past 40 years most refugees have realized that any return will not occur in the immediate future and that it most likely will not mean a return to their original homes. Many now accept "return" to a Palestine state as an alternative, but few refugees today would acknowledge that they have been "resettled."

During the late 1940s and early 1950s, before the international community became aware of refugees' sensitivity to the term, elaborate plans were devised, shifting solution of the problem to resettlement and rehabilitation in the neighboring countries. In 1949, CCP observed that in the long run the refugee problem could be resolved "within the framework of the economic and social rehabilitation of all the countries in the Near East."[82] CCP's Technical Committee on Refugees was instructed to assemble information based on previous studies and make recommendations for refugee repatriation, resettlement, and rehabilitation. The committee called for a double approach: immediate action and a long-range development plan for the region.

A new Economic Survey Mission (ESM) was established by CCP to devise an economic approach; the Technical Committee on Refugees was dissolved and its members were assigned to ESM, which was headed by Gordon R. Clapp, former head of the Tennessee Valley Authority. After surveying all countries where there were large numbers of refugees, ESM reported that there was a possibility of carrying out development projects to facilitate the gradual replacement of refugee relief with a program of public works calculated to improve regional productivity and thus refugee absorption.

The concept of regional economic development was received favorably, and a plan for its implementation, the McGhee plan, was devised by the U.S. State Department. This plan, named after the assistant secretary of state for Near Eastern, African, and South Asian affairs, was linked to repatriation. It was a package deal in which Israel was asked to repatriate 100,000 refugees immediately and to make territorial concessions in exchange for Arab agreement to resettle most of the refugees as part of a regional development scheme. The McGhee Plan was rejected by both Israel and the Arab states, but CCP's recommendations were adopted, and UNRWA was established with finding an economic solution to the refugee problem as one of its major tasks. The General Assembly in 1949–50 approved a $30 million reintegration fund to assist any government in the region requesting funds for projects that would remove refugees from relief.

Since a major reason for establishing ESM was to break the Palestine deadlock through emphasis on an economic approach bypassing complicated political issues, ESM's initial 1949 report included only technical proposals on refugee relief and plans for four small pilot development projects. ESM also recommended reducing relief rolls, which had grown by over 288,000 to 940,000, before January 1950. ESM estimated that $54.9 million would be required to solve the refugee problem within the following 18 months. The task of implementing these proposals was given to the newly established UNRWA.

By the beginning of 1951, at the end of the 18 months targeted for ending relief, only 12,000 of the 878,000 refugees were employed (although corrections in registration had reduced the total number by 60,000). UNRWA had failed in its assigned task to develop works projects to absorb substantial numbers of refugees. Instead, it took over the relief work of the voluntary agencies it replaced; ever since, its principal activity has been as a relief and social welfare organization rather than an agency devoted to developing large-scale works projects for refugee rehabilitation. A renewed attempt to break this cycle was initiated in 1951 with a fresh plan on a much larger scale. The General Assembly proposed a three-year program of major financial support for development in Arab states where it was believed that refugees could be absorbed. A budget of $250 million was planned: $50 million for relief and $200 million for refugee reintegration. Relief was to be progressively reduced over the next three years until only $5 million would be required.

The objective was to eliminate UNRWA by 1954, gradually transferring responsibility for both relief and rehabilitation to the Arab states. Arab cooperation was conditional on retaining absolute guarantees of refugee political rights to compensation and the right to return. Arab states were to contribute land and services for the projects. It was expected that projects for refugee reintegration would parallel programs undertaken for regional development, such as those of the Foreign Operations Administration, the Export-Import Bank, the International Bank for Reconstruction and Development, the British Middle East Office, and the UN Technical Assistance Board.

The keystone of the three-year plan was a scheme to develop the region's water resources, principally the Jordan River system. President Eisenhower delegated Eric Johnston as his special representative in the Middle East to work out political agreements and technical details required to implement the Jordan Valley project. The Johnston plan envisaged the irrigation of over 500,000 *dunums* in Jordan with water from the Yarmuk and Jordan rivers at a total cost of $161,839,000. With increased irrigation and production of electric power, 224,000 workers and their families could be settled in the Jordan Valley: 160,000 would be employed directly in agriculture and 64,000 in ancillary jobs. This would be an increase of 143,000 persons over the number employed in the Jordan Valley during 1953.[83]

The Jordanian government agreed to participate in the Jordan River development scheme, and Johnston succeeded in bridging the gap between Israel and the Arab states over the division of river waters. A technical committee of the Arab League also approved details of the plan. Progress was stalled by Syria's opposition to any project that required direct or indirect cooperation with Israel. In addition to this political obstacle, there were difficulties caused by the land-holding system. Under the existing system, only a handful of individuals with vested interests in the lands affected would benefit.

Before a rational plan could be devised in social as well as in engineering terms, a change in distribution of holdings would have to occur, a change altering the balance of power.

Another major attempt to initiate a project that would relieve Egypt of more than 200,000 refugees in the Gaza Strip involved use of the Nile River to irrigate 120,000 *dunums* in the Sinai Peninsula. Enough water would be siphoned from the Nile under the Suez Canal to irrigate 120,000 *dunums* for the benefit of 60,000 to 70,000 refugees. Studies by UNRWA and the Egyptian government concluded that these refugees could be resettled within five years; those involved could become self-supporting within three to six years after the last refugees were resettled. In June 1953, the Egyptian government signed an agreement with UNRWA that set aside $30 million from UNRWA's rehabilitation fund for projects in Sinai.

By 1955, however, Egypt was emphasizing its own internal development, giving priority to an agricultural development and peasant relocation project in the newly formed "Liberation Province" and to the High Nile Dam at Aswan. Cairo informed UNRWA that development of Liberation Province had progressed more quickly than expected, thereby increasing Egypt's own water requirements. Egypt could not make water available to refugees when it was obliged to restrict the amount of water used by its own citizens. Egypt's answer to the problem was construction of the High Dam. Egypt promised that work could begin on the Sinai project the day work began on the dam. Because of the 1956 Sinai-Suez War and the many political difficulties surrounding construction of the dam, the promise was never kept, and the project faded into obscurity.[84]

Another $30 million from UNRWA's rehabilitation fund was allocated for projects in Syria, according to an agreement signed with UNRWA in October 1952. UNRWA's technical surveys indicated that Syria had the natural resources (land and water) to absorb all the refugees. Under the agreement, UNRWA was to assist in initiating an integrated program of technical training and education and in development of industry, commerce, and agriculture in exchange for public lands to be made available by the government. By the end of 1953, only two small tracts were available, hardly enough to settle more than a few hundred refugees. The quality of the land was so poor that the cost of development for a few refugee families was five times what it would have been in areas withheld from UNRWA. Other state lands more suitable for agriculture held the potential for cheaper and quicker projects; they involved only minor pumping from the Euphrates River. But the Syrian government refused to permit refugee settlement there.[85]

The 1950s was an era of persistent political instability in Syria. It was difficult to obtain commitments from the periodically changing administrations. Four political upheavals between 1947 and 1954 prevented the implementation of any long-term development plans. A tradition of anti-Westernism and suspicion of foreign intervention were added obstacles. Many Syrians questioned the loyalty of the Palestinians, and agreement to resettle any large number of refugees was tantamount to admitting defeat by Israel. In 1950, when Syria's President Shishakli agreed to accept UNRWA's help in absorbing some 82,000 refugees already in the country, public hostility prevented official announcement of the plan for many months.

Although the Litani River area in Lebanon had been designated by ESM as the site for one of its four pilot projects, all UN development plans for refugee rehabilitation there were abandoned. The Lebanese government's official reason was that the country was already overpopulated and had no room for additional settlers. Lebanon's demographic problem—the balance between Christians and Muslims—was the principal obstacle to progress. The attitude toward refugees was so unaccommodating that they were refused not only citizenship but even official work permits.

In November 1952, UNRWA concluded an agreement with the Libyan government to resettle 1,200 families who in due course would be given the rights and privileges of Libyan citizens. The cost of this program was estimated at $2 million, but the agreement was never fully implemented. Only a small number of artisans were permitted to settle in Libya.

Iraq was also seen as an area for potential large-scale refugee resettlement in the 1950s. Its vast land and water resources were still undeveloped, and the country was considered underpopulated.

Although surveys indicated that large numbers of refugees could be absorbed, political obstacles in the country and the adamant opposition of the refugees themselves prevented any agreement to use money from the rehabilitation fund in Iraq.

The objective of the UN's three-year program and the rehabilitation fund was to liquidate international financial responsibility for the refugee problem, but by 1954 not even 8,000 Palestinians had been made self-sufficient by the effort. Less than 5 percent of the $200 million allocated for reintegration had been used and no major development project was under way. Instead of terminating UNRWA, the General Assembly extended its mandate for five more years, to June 1960, and added more funds for relief grants.

The three governments that signed agreements with UNRWA for large-scale development projects—Jordan, Egypt, and Syria—maintained their opposition to resettlement. UNRWA's acting director in 1954 reported that the Palestinians "appreciate that the facilities offered to the refugees are no more than temporary, and that the acceptance by a refugee of a house and an opportunity to resume a normal life does not in any way affect or reduce his right to repatriation or compensation when the time comes."[86] The refugees actively opposed the program, submitting frequent petitions and manifestos rejecting resettlement. UNRWA alone could do little to change these attitudes, and no Arab government felt strong enough to challenge either the refugees or public opinion.

In a last effort at an economic approach, the United States called on UN secretary general Dag Hammarskjöld during 1959 to initiate a study to determine whether capital investment in large-scale projects could produce enough jobs to end refugee reliance on international assistance. In his report to the General Assembly, Hammarskjöld observed that the unemployed refugees should be regarded not as a liability but as an asset for the future, a reservoir of labor to assist in raising the living standards of the whole region. The report called for resettlement of refugees in "the areas where they now live" and appealed to Arab host countries to cooperate in expanding rehabilitation programs to enable the refugees to support themselves without UNRWA assistance.[87]

The proposal was rejected at a Palestinian conference convened in Beirut during June 1959; conference participants labeled the plan an "imperialist move through United Nations institutions to dissolve the Palestinian people into the economy of the Middle East." Jordan verbally rejected the proposal but formed a five-member committee to study it. However, the committee never issued a formal rejection statement.[88] Representatives of ten Arab countries replied to the UN secretary-general that the refugee problem was not an economic one; the UN would have to continue its responsibility for the refugees until it could "take the necessary measures for the implementation of its resolutions providing for the return of the refugees."[89] This was the last overt attempt to approach the problem through large-scale internationally financed projects for refugee resettlement.

The Israeli government appointed a ministerial commission in August 1982 to deal with the refugee issue. The commission was headed by Mordechai Ben-Porat, minister without portfolio. The commission included David Levy, housing minister; Moshe Arens, defense minister; Yitzhak Shamir, foreign minister; Moshe Nissim, justice minister; Yaacov Meridor, economics minister; and Yuval Ne'eman, science minister, assisted by a team of experts.

The commission's report emphasized the dual nature of the refugee problem, stating that "the two groups [Arab and Jewish refugees] are roughly the same in size, and their cases are clearly interrelated." The Arab states were held responsible for both problems. Furthermore, the report charged that the Arab states were hindering attempts to integrate the refugees into their societies.[90]

The commission asserted that Israel had already contributed to alleviation of the problem by facilitating the return of more than 40,000 Arab refugees under its family-reunion program and permitting another 70,000 to reunite with their families in the West Bank and Gaza. The report maintained that after 1970 more than 50,000 Gaza refugees, about a quarter of the camp dwellers in the area, had been resettled "in new and superior housing facilities." But such rehabilitation efforts had been hampered by the PLO's "negative influence" in the West Bank.

The commission's conclusions and recommendations were as follows: (1) A clear-cut separation between the political and the economic and social aspects of the Palestine refugee problem was called for. (2) Although political aspects could be resolved only as part of a peace agreement, immediate progress could be achieved in economic and social matters as they related to refugees in areas under Israeli control. (3) "In the spirit of the age-old Jewish heritage," Israel had evolved "a comprehensive programme of action designed to rehabilitate the refugees in their areas of residence, within the shortest possible time." (4) To assist the refugees in becoming "fully part of the society in which they live," they would be aided in obtaining "proper housing," "all essential services," and an opportunity "to work their own plot of land or to engage in other productive employment."[91]

This was to be a five-year rehabilitation program focusing on the establishment of new housing and the allotment of land and financial assistance to enable refugees to build their own homes under a government master plan. Health and welfare services in the West Bank would be unified and UNRWA's educational facilities would be integrated into the national school network. All of these steps would be undertaken "in full coordination with UNRWA."

The Arab states would be called upon to "act decisively to absorb their own brethren in their midst." A special ministerial committee would be established to deal separately with claims against the Arab countries by Jewish refugees. Financing for this project, to be obtained "from various international sources," was estimated at $1.5 billion.[92] According to Ben-Porat, implementation of the plan "would depend on the rate at which outside funds for it would arrive in Israel." Israel had already made substantial contributions to resolution of the problem, according to Ben-Porat, by absorbing some 1,250,000 Jewish refugees from Arab countries, by "accepting back into the country an additional 110,000 Palestinian Arabs in the framework of family reunification programs," and by contributions to UNRWA over the years totaling $12 million.[93]

This plan was, in essence, a reiteration of Israel's basic position on the refugee issue. It placed blame on the Arab states, equated the Palestine Arab refugee problem with the issue of Jewish refugees from Arab countries, offered to move refugees under its jurisdiction from camps to outside housing, and called for international financing of such projects. Neither the United States, the Arab states, nor the UN pursued the offer further, and yet another unfulfilled official plan was added to the collection.

Recent Developments

The Gulf War intensified problems of refugee rehabilitation, especially in Jordan, where the largest number of refugees are located and on which major plans for resettlement have focused. Jordan's economy had already been deteriorating prior to the war. After a high growth rate and prosperity in the 1970s and early 1980s, the economy was hit by recession. Remittances from Jordanians (many of them Palestinians) working abroad decreased greatly. The government was forced to reschedule its foreign debt, and under an agreement with the International Monetary Fund it sharply reduced food subsidies. Between 1987 and 1989, living standards fell by 22 percent, accompanied by a 26 percent increase in inflation. After a period of full employment between the mid-1970s and early 1980s, unemployment shot upward. By late 1991, the unemployment rate was between 20 and 25 percent, compared with 3.6 percent in the early 1980s.

The Gulf crisis brought economic life in Jordan to a standstill. The influx of several hundred thousand returning Jordanian-Palestinians aggravated the setback caused by the loss of tourism, decline in trade at Akaba port, and an end to financial aid from the Gulf states. Jordan also lost two of its best markets, Iraq and Kuwait. All remittances from the Gulf were halted. The World Bank estimated that in the year after the crisis began, Jordan lost about $3 billion in remittances, exports, tourism, and transportation fees. A survey by UNICEF in 1991 stated that the number of people in Jordan at or below the poverty line increased to nearly 33 percent as a result of the crisis.[94]

The great majority of Palestinians leaving Kuwait had Jordanian passports and were legally Jordanian subjects, and therefore were not refugees in a technical sense. However, they had lived in Kuwait for many years; their homes, property, bank accounts, and jobs were in Kuwait, not in Jordan. Many left Kuwait with unpaid wages, lost end-of-service and retirement benefits, and savings accounts either destroyed in Kuwait or inaccessible in Iraqi, Kuwaiti, or Saudi Arabian banks. Homes and personal belongings were stolen or abandoned; commercial property and business assets were also lost. Many had raised their families in Kuwait, and among the refugees who were legally Jordanian were thousands who had never been in the Hashemite Kingdom of Jordan.

Jordan was ill-prepared to receive this sudden influx, which was nearly equal to 10 percent of its population. By December 1990, the Palestinian-Jordanian refugee population constituted about one-third of the total number of refugees who came from the Gulf. About 500,000 of the 750,000 refugees left for their countries of origin, but the 250,000 to 300,000 Palestinians had no other place to give them even temporary refuge.

By some estimates, about half of the unemployed Palestinians were college or university graduates. Many of them had studied in the hope of finding employment in the Gulf. But with Kuwait's policy of ridding the country of Palestinians, the declining economies of other Gulf states, and their policies of placing their own citizens in jobs formerly held by foreigners, there was little hope for outsiders to find work in the region.

The Gulf refugee problem has threatened Jordan's development plans. The recent influx is expected to double domestic shortages of water and overwhelm transportation, communication, health, and sewage services. As result of the refugee influx, the objective of Jordan's economic planning has changed from promoting growth and prosperity to minimizing the deterioration of living standards and maintaining the already precarious quality of life. The cost of even this modest objective has been estimated by Jordanian authorities at between $3.7 and $4.5 billion.

As a result of the refugee influx there has been a temporary construction boom in Jordan that was the basis of an unusually high rate of economic growth, about 10 percent, during the latter part of 1991 and early 1992; 1992 was the first year in a decade to achieve a growth rate higher than the rate of population increase. Housing construction also generated an increase in ancillary factories producing cement, steel bars, wood, and furniture, and in the quarrying and trucking industries. The growth in construction was a factor in lowering unemployment from 24 percent in 1991 to below 20 percent in 1992. However, this construction boom cannot continue for long, and when the pace decreases the country will again face the need for economic growth and jobs for the rapidly increasing population.

In January 1992, Jordan's King Hussein proposed that the burden of unemployed Palestinians be spread among the Arab states through the device of dual nationality. If host countries permitted their refugees to hold Palestinian as well as host country nationality, the burden would be more fairly distributed. With compensation expected for property lost in Palestine, economic integration into the host countries would be facilitated, said the king. Other host countries should follow Jordan's example and grant the refugees citizenship because a Palestinian state in the West Bank and Gaza could not possibly absorb several million diaspora Palestinians. "Is it reasonable that Israelis should enjoy the right to have Israeli nationality and the nationality of another country while the situation of the Palestine Arabs in the Arab world remains unchanged?" the king asked.[95]

Large-scale, high-cost development plans to resettle the Palestine refugees have not succeeded because many of the obstacles that existed in 1950 when ESM investigated prospects for regional economic reconstruction still exist. In the words of ESM's final report: "The region is not ready, the projects are not ready, the people and Governments are not ready, for large-scale development of the region's basic river systems or major undeveloped land areas."[96] While financial resources in the region have become much more accessible as a result of the oil revolution in the 1970s and 1980s, political squabbles have blocked inter-Arab cooperation. International financing is much more difficult to obtain because of the economic recession that has spread throughout the world and the demands of many other refugee crises.

But the situation is not entirely dark. As far back as 1950, UNRWA observed that individual refugees, when offered opportunities to take advantage of minor projects, were eager to become economically independent and leave the camps. A number of small-scale successes occurred, mostly in Jordan. In Amman, an urban development provided housing for a few hundred refugees. UNRWA also provided 80 percent of the capital to establish the Jordan Development Bank, which extended loans to several thousand refugees for small-business and commercial purposes until the bank was dissolved in 1966–67.[97]

Small projects focusing on individual refugees were not burdened by the psychological obstacles associated with massive works schemes. The threat of insecurity awaiting a person removed from ration rolls or a refugee camp in exchange for a farm, workshop, or new business where opportunities for making a living were clearly visible seemed far less than the risk in store for a mass of people moved to some unfamiliar region where the physical realities of life were uncertain. Arab governments and refugee leaders were inclined to lend support to the small-project approach, which was not stigmatized with the label of "resettlement," a term that was considered synonymous with defeat by Israel and abandonment of the right of return. UNRWA's work with refugee retraining and its new income-generating projects (see "The Future of UNRWA and the Refugees" below) have underscored the success of an individual rather than a mass approach to rehabilitation.

UNRWA's Transformation

Since its establishment in 1949, UNRWA has shifted its emphasis from relief to preparing Palestinian refugees for the exigencies of daily life in their immediate surroundings. UNRWA's education programs, particularly the establishment of vocational training institutions, have focused on providing the refugees with the skills to free them from dependence on international assistance.

The portion of the agency's 1990–91 budget allotted to relief and social services had declined to less than 11 percent. About half of the budget was devoted to education, 18 percent to health services, and the rest to operations and common services, including items such as transportation and rent for land where refugee camps are situated.[98]

The education budget finances more than 640 elementary and junior secondary schools with over 390,000 pupils, eight vocational and teachers' training centers with places for more than 5,100, and almost 750 annual university scholarships (see table 1). The education staff (11,500 persons) constitutes more than half the total number of UNRWA employees. More than 90 percent of UNRWA employees are Palestinian; fewer than 200 of the total 19,000 are non-Middle Easterners.[99]

Since the refugee population grows by about 3 percent annually, substantial increases are required to keep up with ever-greater demands for new teachers, additional classrooms, and school equipment. The number of pupils will grow to over 400,000, and more than 1,000 new teachers will be needed in the two-year period after 1990–91.

UNRWA schools now operate on a very economical basis. The overall student:teacher ratio is 38:1 at the elementary level, and 28:1 at the preparatory level. The annual cost per student is about $270 per elementary student and $350 at the preparatory level, low by both regional and international levels.

During the 1950s and 1960s, when there was greater emphasis on works programs, vocational training was started. Since the first vocational training center was opened at Kalandia near Jerusalem in 1953, thousands of refugee men and women have been trained as pharmacy assistants, laboratory technicians, office workers, dental hygienists, hairdressers, electricians, auto mechanics, and metal and construction workers. During the era of rapid economic growth following the oil revolution of the 1970s, thousands of these trainees found employment in the Gulf. Many worked there for years, sending remittances to families remaining in the host countries.

At present, some 4,700 students, 20 percent of them women, receive vocational and teacher training at eight UNRWA centers in Jordan, Lebanon, Syria, Gaza, and the West Bank. However, with the decline of income from oil and the slowed pace of development, job opportunities decreased. Economic decline was intensified by the Gulf war, with the result that trainees are now experiencing difficulty in finding employment. After the outbreak of the Intifada in 1987 and Israel's adoption of severe measures to repress it, UNRWA adopted a protective role in the West Bank and Gaza refugee camps. When Israel imposed lengthy curfews and resorted to mass arrests, the use of tear gas, and other forceful measures, UNRWA designated several of its international staff, mostly Europeans and North Americans, to observe the situation and if possible to defuse potentially violent confrontations between camp residents and the Israeli military. This function soon became institutionalized and the UNRWA observers, called refugee affairs officers, became an integral part of the staff. This new protective function was similar to the role of the UN high commissioner for refugees in other refugee situations.

The Future of UNRWA and the Refugees

UNRWA commissioner-general Ilter Turkmen observed in his November 1991 report to the UN that the agency and its activities were at a turning point corresponding to changes in the Palestine question. The opening of peace negotiations between Israel and its neighbors and with the Palestinians, he said, was a harbinger of new thinking about the refugee problem and about the role of the agency.[100]

New developments in the relationships between Israel and the Arab world will inevitably lead to changes in the status of the Palestine Arab refugees. Turkmen predicted that when the refugee problem is resolved in the West Bank and Gaza, "the Agency will be dissolved, transferring its facilities, structures and services to the emerging Palestinian institutions. That day will be for UNRWA not a day of sorrow but a day of completion and achievement." UNRWA's 19,000 Palestinian staff and their services would find "their place in the new administrative structures, and their services will be needed even more in the new environment."[101]

Graduates of UNRWA's schools and training centers would continue to serve their community and the schools, clinics, training centers, and hospitals established by the agency, but under new management. The commissioner-general's statement implied that although UNRWA may cease to exist after a peace settlement, its personnel and the infrastructure they have created will become an invaluable asset in the reconstruction of a new Middle East. To realize this aspiration, UNRWA will have to reorient its activities before it is dissolved and its facilities are transferred to a new Palestinian authority.

There are indications that attention is already being given to reorientation; one is the new program of "income generation" instituted in 1990. At first, the program was intended to assist special hardship cases brought about by the uprising in the Occupied Territories. Initially, small grants were provided to "hardship families" for small businesses such as well drilling, hairdressing, clothing manufacturing, and printing.[102]

In 1991 UNRWA decided to supplement grants with low-interest loans to finance self-help projects intended to create jobs for Palestinians with skills. Financing would come from a revolving fund using monies contributed by donors. The objective was to support local economies through the development of small business and micro-enterprises in industry and agriculture. The main goal was to generate income by creating jobs and to enhance local self-sufficiency. Another goal was to assist women in establishing small businesses and microenterprises.[103]

Hand in hand with the disbursement of loans to encourage the creation of jobs, UNRWA planned to offer training in small business management to remedy the "lack of general entrepreneurial and labour-management skills" in the Palestinian economies, particularly the Occupied Territories. To succeed, it would be necessary to reorient many who had been educated in a system that produced a large number of bureaucrats and to place far greater emphasis on self-reliance.

The focus on small- and medium-scale industrial and business enterprises within the framework of balanced development was also emphasized at a meeting convened by the ESCWA in Amman in December 1991. However, the experts observed, for such enterprises to succeed, it would be necessary to enhance all types and sizes of enterprises in all productive sectors of the economy. They noted that stressing small- and medium-sized enterprises in a stagnant economy could lead to their early failure.[104]

UNRWA officials observed that Palestinians preferred this type of assistance to conventional relief. Transition from a welfare to a developmental philosophy had been tried successfully on a small scale in other Third World countries. Now, rather than large-scale development schemes like those projected for the Middle East during the 1950s and 1960s, the emphasis would be on microdevelopment, planning, and training.

Local banks were designated to administer the new loan funds, after UNRWA staff undertook field studies to determine project feasibility and approved applications to the banks. The program was well received by both European donors and potential Palestinian borrowers, with the result that UNRWA embarked on a five-year program to raise $20 million for the loans. The program has now been extended to Jordan, Syria, and Lebanon. During the 1992–93 fiscal year, $8 million should be raised to finance the income generation scheme for an estimated 2,700 families in all the host areas.

The amount of funding provided for income generation and the number of refugees directly affected may seem minute in the context of UNRWA's overall operations; however, the new approach is a first step in the transition of UNRWA from an international relief organization administered by non-Palestinians to a developmental agency run and managed by Palestinians.

At present, international assistance to the refugees is motivated more by political than humanitarian considerations. According to some officials, the resources and employment provided by UNRWA are major factors in maintaining political stability in the host countries; in some host countries UNRWA is the second largest employer after the government. As Ilter Turkmen emphasized:

> The services UNRWA has provided to the Palestine refugees and, on occasion, to others in need, are the type of services which are normally provided to various beneficiary groups by governments, sometimes with assistance from appropriate United Nations agencies and programmes. UNRWA was created solely for Palestine refugees because of the historical context of the Palestine problem.
> UNRWA is therefore a symbol of the international commitment to the Palestinian people, a reflection of the fact that their refugee status was different than that of other refugees, that they should benefit from

the international community's assistance until the problem was resolved, that their case was not a simple one of resettlement in a third country or integration in the country of first asylum.[105]

Today, as refugee crises proliferate throughout the world, demands on contributing nations have so increased that they will be forced to compare the needs of Palestinian refugees with the needs of refugees in places like Sudan, Somalia, Cambodia, Eastern Europe, and the Balkans. When comparisons are made, the quarter of a billion dollars provided yearly for the Palestinians places them at great advantage. If there is an Arab-Israeli peace settlement, pressures will mount to terminate this relatively large per capita aid program or at least to make it more commensurate with assistance other refugees receive.

UNRWA's role, either as a relief or a welfare organization, will no longer generate the support it has received for over 40 years. The agency could, as suggested by Turkmen, turn over its facilities and personnel to a new Palestinian entity and to the respective host countries, or it could be transformed into an organization dependent less on voluntary contributions than on developmental loans through one or more of the various international development funds such as the World Bank.

Finally, the Palestine Arab refugee problem cannot be resolved except as part of an overall settlement of the Arab-Israeli conflict. Issues such as the political identity and status of Palestinians, whether as citizens of a new Palestinian entity or as permanent residents in the host countries, will be determined within the context of agreements between Israel and its neighbors. The outcome of disputes over Jerusalem, where there are three UNRWA camps (Shu'fat, Jalazone, Kalandia) will determine the legal status of more than 100,000 refugees (20,000 in camps). The economic future of tens of thousands of refugees will be influenced by agreements on compensation. The types, amounts, and forms of payment and evaluation of property are to be determined within the context of a peace settlement.

The extent to which programs like the income generation scheme succeed in diminishing refugee reliance on outside assistance will depend in large measure on the success or failure of regional economic planning. At present, there are no realistic detailed plans for regional development. Even the schemes of individual countries where refugees might settle are not based on credible surveys and calculations. Before regional projects can even be planned, there must be agreement on an equitable allocation of resources, the most important of which is water.

Since World War II, several plans have been devised for the allocation and cooperative development of water resources in Israel/Palestine, Jordan, Syria, Lebanon, and Egypt. However, the schemes have foundered because the parties concerned have failed to reach political accord. Agreement on water sources, the key to regional economic development, must be preceded by a peace settlement satisfactory to all those countries whose cooperation is vital. These countries include not only Israel and its Arab neighbors but also Turkey, because of its potential as a major water source for all geographic Syria.

The multilateral functional discussions on refugees, water, economic development, environment, and security that are part of the new Middle East peace process demonstrate the participants' awareness that these issues are interlinked and important for regional stability. The functional discussions can provide a catalyst, a stimulant to further progress, by demonstrating the urgent and interrelated nature of these problems. But to achieve progress in coping with specific issues, there must be further progress in the bilateral discussions; without such progress, it will be difficult, if not impossible, to reach agreement on the many functional problems. However, if the Palestine refugee problem is not resolved and the number of refugees continues to grow at the present rapid rate, they will become an ever increasing source of instability in the Middle East. Although the plight of the Palestine refugees is not as severe as that of refugees in places such as Somalia, Sudan, and the Balkans, the political consequences of their situation could be far more disastrous, for they are dispersed through some of the most sensitive parts of the Middle East. As the refugees become increasingly radicalized because of their growing unrest and disenchantment with Middle Eastern governments, they become the carriers of ideologies such as those of Hamas, which threaten the stability of the region as a whole.

Notes

1. UNRWA, *UNRWA 1950–1990: Serving Palestine Refugees* (Vienna, April 1990, mimeographed), 6.

2. Ibid.

3. UN Conciliation Commission for Palestine, *Final Report of the United Nations Economic Survey Mission for the Middle East*, pt. 1: "An Approach to Economic Development in the Middle East" (New York, December 28, 1949), 3.

4. UNRWA, *UNRWA 1950–1990*, 6.

5. *Population Bulletin of ESCWA* (UN Economic and Social Commission for West Asia) no. 27 (Baghdad, December 1985).

6. UNRWA, *UNRWA 1950–1990*, 6.

7. For official UNRWA population figures, see UN General Assembly, Official Records, *Annual Report of the Commissioner-General of the United Nations Relief and Works Agency for Palestine Refugees in the Near East (UNRWA)*.

8. U.S. Bureau of the Census, Center for International Research, *Palestinian Projections for 16 Countries/Areas of the World 1990 to 2010* (Washington, D.C., March 1991, mimeographed), 52. The last Palestine government census prior to the end of the Mandate, taken in 1931, reported 759,700 Muslims, 174,606 Jews, and 88,907 Christians. The last official estimate in 1944 reported 1,061,277 Muslims, 553,600 Jews, and 135,547 Christians (Palestine Government, *Survey of Palestine 1945–1946*, vol. 1, chap. 6, table 1, 141). Estimates for May 1948 based on these figures indicate that 1,380,000 Arabs, 700,000 Jews, and 35,000 others resided in Palestine at the end of the Mandate.

9. UN General Assembly, *Annual Report of the Commissioner-General of UNRWA 1 July 1966–30 June 1967* (New York: United Nations, 1967), suppl. 13 (A/6713), 1ff.

10. U.S. Bureau of the Census, *Palestinian Projections*; UNRWA, *UNRWA General Information Sheet* (Vienna, April 1992); Palestine Academic Society for the Study of International Affairs, *1992 Diary-Yearbook* (Jerusalem, 1992), 152–164.

11. U.S. Bureau of the Census, *Palestinian Projections*, 57. Numbers have been rounded to the nearest thousand.

12. Ibid., 56.

13. UNRWA, *UNRWA 1950–1990*, 6–7.

14. Shawn Tully, "The Big Moneymen of Palestine Inc.," *Fortune*, July 31, 1989, 176–186.

15. *Population Bulletin of ESCWA* no. 27, 82–83.

16. Ibid., 83–84.

17. Sadek J. Al-Azm, "Palestinian Zionism," *Die Welt des Islams* 28 (1988): 91.

18. Al-Azm, "Palestinian Zionism," 91.

19. Rosemary Sayigh, "The Palestinian Experience: Integration and Non-Integration in the Arab Ghourba," *Arab Studies Quarterly* 1, no. 2 (Spring 1979): 106.

20. *FBIS* [Foreign Broadcast Information Service] *Daily Report: Near East and South Asia*, March 17, 1992 (FBIS-NES-92-052, 7–9), from the *Jordan Times* (in English), March 16, 1992, 1 and 5.

21. Musa Samha, "Migration of Refugees and Non-Refugees to Amman 1948–1977," *Population Bulletin of ESCWA* no. 19 (Baghdad, December 1980), 56.

22. Palestinian National Council (PNC), political communiqué, reprinted in *Journal of Palestine Studies* 17, no. 2 (Winter 1988): 216–223.

23. *FBIS Daily Report: Near East and South Asia*, March 19, 1992 (FBIS-NES-92-054, 3), from *Akhbar Al-Usubu'*, March 19, 1992, and Algiers Voice of Palestine radio broadcast, March 18, 1992.

24. Laurie A. Brand, *Palestinians in the Arab World: Institution Building and the Search for State* (New York: Columbia University Press, 1988), 111–112.

25. Sharon S. Russell, "Politics and Ideology in Migration Policy Formulation: The Case of Kuwait," *International Migration Review* 23, no. 1 (Spring 1989): 32.

26. Ibid., 35.

27. Brand, 113–114.

28. Russell, 38.

29. Brand, 115–116.

30. Ibid., 122–125.

31. Ibid., 108.

32. *Middle East International*, July 27, 1991, 39.

33. *FBIS Daily Report: Near East and South Asia*, September 19, 1991, 22; *World Refugee Survey 1991* (Washington, D.C.: U.S. Committee for Refugees, 1991), 93.

34. *Mideast Mirror*, February 3, 1992, 92.

35. *Middle East International*, June 28, 1991, 3.

36. *Mideast Mirror*, January 15, 1992, 4.

37. Nasser H. Aruri and Samih Farsoun, "Palestinian Communities and Arab Host Countries," in *The Sociology of the Palestinians*, ed. Khalil Nakleh and Elia Zureik (New York: St. Martin's Press, 1980), 131.

38. UN General Assembly, *Annual Report of the Director of UNRWA Covering the Period 1 July 1951 to 30 June 1952* (New York: United Nations, 1952), 45–46.

39. See Rex Brynen, *Sanctuary and Survival: The PLO in Lebanon* (Boulder, Colo.: Westview Press, 1990), 48–52, and appendix, "The Cairo Agreement (1969)," 201–202.

40. Rashid Khalidi, "The Palestinians in Lebanon: Social Repercussions of Israel's Invasion," *Middle East Journal* 38, no. 2 (Spring 1984): 255.

41. Personal communication on the socioeconomic situation of Palestinians in Gaza, West Bank, Jordan, and Lebanon by a United Nations source, 1991.

42. Ibid.

43. Avi Shlaim, "Husni Za'im and the Plan to Resettle Palestinian Refugees in Syria," *Journal of Palestine Studies* 15, no. 4 (Summer 1986): 68–80.

44. *Annual Report of the Director of UNRWA . . . 1952*, 46–48.

45. U.S. Department of State, *Foreign Relations of the United States 1948*, vol. 5, pt. 2 (Washington, D.C., 1976), 1404.

46. Nadav Avner, *Will There Always Be Refugees? A Survey and Proposals for a Solution of the Middle East Refugee Problem* (Jerusalem: Israel Information Center, 1985), 41–42.

47. *The Forward* (New York), June 5, 1992.

48. Kurt René Radley, "The Palestinian Refugees: The Right to Return in International Law," *American Journal of International Law* 72, no. 3 (July 1978): 600–601.

49. Palestinian Declaration of Independence and PNC Political Communiqué, reprinted in *Journal of Palestine Studies* 17, no. 2 (Winter 1988): 213–223.

50. Charles L. Geddes (ed.), *A Documentary History of the Arab-Israeli Conflict* (New York: Praeger, 1991), 322.

51. Rashid I. Khalidi, "Observations of the Right of Return," *Journal of Palestine Studies* 21, no. 2 (Winter 1992): 29–40.

52. Vivian A. Bull, *The West Bank: Is It Viable?* (Lexington, Mass.: D. C. Heath, 1975), 12–13.

53. Brian Van Arkadie, *Benefits and Burdens: A Report on the West Bank and Gaza Strip Economies Since 1967* (Washington, D.C.: Carnegie Endowment for International Peace, 1977), 153–154.

54. For a discussion of Israeli policies, see Meron Benvenisti, *The West Bank Data Project: A Survey of Israel's Policies* (Washington, D.C.: American Enterprise Institute for Public Policy Research, 1984); Benvenisti, *The West Bank Handbook: A Political Lexicon* (Jerusalem: Jerusalem Post, 1986); Don Peretz, *Intifada: The Palestinian Uprising* (Boulder, Colo.: Westview Press, 1990), chap. 3.

55. Personal communication by a UN source, 1991.

56. Benvenisti, *The West Bank Handbook*, 2.

57. Van Arkadie, *Benefits and Burdens*, 45.

58. Personal communication by a UN source, 1991.

59. U.S. State Department, Office of Legislative Affairs, "Israeli Settlements in the Occupied Territories," May 1, 1992, cited in *Journal of Palestine Studies* 21, no. 4 (Summer 1992): 171–172. According to this report, about half the land in the West Bank has been dedicated by Israeli authorities for Israeli use, although Jewish settlements occupy only a fraction of the West Bank area closed to Arab use. About one-third of the Gaza area has been reserved for Israeli use.

60. George T. Abed, *The Economic Viability of a Palestinian State* (Washington, D.C.: Institute for Palestine Studies, 1990), 16.

61. Ibid., 6.

62. Ibid., 6.

63. Ibid., 37.

64. Ibid., 7.

65. Center for Engineering and Planning, *Masterplanning: The State of Palestine, Suggested Guidelines*, prepared for ANERA (Ramallah, West Bank, 1992), 3.

66. Ibid., 134–135.

67. Personal communication by a UN source, 1991.

68. Abed, *Economic Viability*, x.

69. Center for Engineering and Planning, *Masterplanning*, 135.

70. Ibid., 59.

71. Ibid., 55.

72. *Journal of Palestine Studies* 20, no. 4 (Summer 1991), 172.

73. Don Peretz, *Israel and the Palestine Arabs* (New York: AMS Press, 1958), 143.

74. Ibid., 144–145.

75. "The Other Refugees—Jews from Arab Countries: Their Claims," *Newsview* 4, no. 63 (November 29, 1983): 18. According to Israeli estimates, half the 30,000 Jewish families in Iraq owned buildings estimated to be worth 30 million Israeli pounds (LI); Jewish lands were worth LI 5 million; synagogues, schools, and other communal buildings were worth another LI 2 million. Movable property was unevenly distributed. About 9,000 families had property worth LI 750 each, and 12,000 families had assets of LI 2,000 each. There were 100 families with fortunes of LI 150,000 each and 50 families with fortunes of LI 300,000 each. At the time the Israeli pound was approximately equal in value to the British pound (*Jerusalem Post*, May 23, 1950).

76. UN General Assembly, Official Records (6th session) suppl. 18, 1951, 17–19.

77. Peretz, *Israel and the Palestine Arabs*, 218.

78. Don Peretz, "Problems of Arab Refugee Compensation," *Middle East Journal* 8, no. 4 (Autumn 1954): 414.

79. Ibid.

80. Sami Hadawi, *Palestinian Rights and Losses in 1948: A Comprehensive Study*, pt. 5: "An Economic Assessment of Total Palestinian Losses" by Atef Kubursi (London, 1988).

81. Peretz, "Problems of Arab Refugee Compensation," 415.

82. Peretz, *Israel and the Palestine Arabs*, chap. 4.

83. Peretz, *Israel and the Palestine Arabs*, 21.

84. Ibid., 24.

85. Ibid., 25–26.

86. Ibid., 21.

87. Milton Viorst, *Reaching for the Olive Branch: UNRWA and Peace in the Middle East* (Bloomington, Ind.: Indiana University Press, 1989), 38.

88. M. Abdul Hadi, *The Palestine Question and Peaceful Solutions: 1934–74* (Sidon, Lebanon, 1975).

89. Viorst, *Reaching for the Olive Branch*, 39.

90. The Ministerial Commission for Solving the Middle East Refugee Problem, *On Middle East Refugees—Ministerial Report* (Jerusalem, November 1983).

91. Ibid., 4–5.

92. Ibid.

93. U.S. Department of State, unclassified incoming telegram from Tel Aviv, October 1983.

94. "Jordan Struggles to Cope with Refugee Influx," *Jordan Issues and Perspectives* (Jordan Information Bureau, Washington, D.C.) no. 10 (April–May 1992): 3; Brewster Grace and Wafa Suliman, "Palestinian Returnees to Jordan Inadvertent Victims of the Gulf War," *Quaker Middle East Representatives* (Amman), September 1991; Eliahu Kanofsky, *The Economic Consequences of the Persian Gulf War: Accelerating OPEC's Demise*, Policy Papers no. 30 (Washington, D.C.: Washington Institute for Near East Policy, 1992), draft.

95. *Mideast Mirror*, January 15, 1992, 4.

96. UN Conciliation Commission for Palestine, *Final Report of the United Nations Economic Survey Mission*, pt. 1, p. 3.

97. Peretz, *Israel and the Palestine Arabs*, 12.

98. UNRWA, *UNRWA 1950–1990*, 29; UN General Assembly, *Annual Report of the Commissioner-General of UNRWA 1 July 1990–30 June 1991* (New York: United Nations, 1991).

99. The information in this paragraph and the rest of this section came from interviews with UNRWA officials and the reports cited above.

100. UNRWA, "Statement by Mr. Ilter Turkmen, Commissioner-General of UNRWA, to the Special Political Committee of the General Assembly," November 15, 1991.

101. Ibid.

102. Personal communication by a UN source, 1991.

103. Ibid.

104. UNECOSOC, ESCWA, *Expert Group Meeting on the Absorption of Returnees in the ESCWA Region With Special Emphasis on Opportunities in the Industrial Sector: Summary and Main Recommendations* (Amman, December 1991).

105. UNRWA, "Statement by Ilter Turkmen."

Index

Jennings Randolph Program for

International Peace

As part of the statute establishing the United States Institute of Peace, Congress envisioned a fellowship program that would appoint "scholars and leaders of peace from the United States and abroad to pursue scholarly inquiry and other appropriate forms of communication on international peace and conflict resolution." The program was named after Senator Jennings Randolph of West Virginia, whose efforts over four decades helped to establish the Institute.

Since it began in 1987, the Jennings Randolph Program has played a key role in the Institute's effort to build a national center of research, dialogue, and education on critical problems of conflict and peace. Through a rigorous annual competition, outstanding men and women from diverse nations and fields are selected to carry out projects designed to expand and disseminate knowledge on violent international conflict and the wide range of ways it can be peacefully managed or resolved.

The Institute's Distinguished Fellows and Peace Fellows are individuals from a wide variety of academic and other professional backgrounds who work at the Institute on research and education projects they have proposed and participate in the Institute's collegial and public outreach activities. The Institute's Peace Scholars are doctoral candidates at American universities who are working on their dissertations.

Institute fellows and scholars have worked on such varied subjects as international negotiation, regional security arrangements, conflict resolution techniques, international legal systems, ethnic and religious conflict, arms control, and the protection of human rights. These issues have been examined in settings throughout the world, including the former Soviet Union, Europe, Latin America, sub-Saharan Africa, and South Asia.

As part of its effort to disseminate original and useful analyses of peace and conflict to policymakers and the public, the Institute publishes book manuscripts and other written products that result from the fellowship work and meet the Institute's high standards of quality.

Michael S. Lund
Director

$\mathcal{P}$ALESTINIANS, REFUGEES,
and the
MIDDLE EAST PEACE PROCESS

$\mathcal{T}$he text of this book is
set in Janson; the display type is Futura.
Cover design by Supon Design Group; in-
terior design by Joan Engelhardt and Day
Wilkes Dosch; map prepared by Marie
Marr-Williams; page makeup by Helene Y.
Redmond of HYR Graphics.